MEET
Deborah Newton

Since she sold her first sweater in 1982 to McCALL's magazine, Deborah Newton has designed and produced hundreds, maybe thousands, of knitted garments of all types which have earned her a reputation as one of the top knitwear designers in the United States. Her earlier career as a creator of stage costumes has endowed her work with a dramatic flair and elements of fine tailoring. In 1992, she distilled her experience and knowledge into a book, DESIGNING KNITWEAR (Taunton Press), an invaluable guide for amateur knitters who wish to create original patterns or simply improve their skills. The book remains in print nearly twenty years later, having attained the status of a classic. Deborah's work continues to appear in magazines and in book form. She designed the sweaters for another Leisure Arts Publication — DEBORAH NEWTON'S CABLE COLLECTION. She also designs knitted fabrics for the Seventh Avenue garment trade.

Born in Rhode Island, she has been a resident of Providence for over thirty years, where she lives with author Paul Di Filippo, her cocker spaniel Brownie, and her cat Penny Century. Perhaps her favorite place to relax in the world is the picturesque ocean haven of Block Island, although she admits that she has never yet designed a knitted bathing suit.

Choice & Care of Yarns
FOR WARM WEATHER SWEATERS

All the yarns used for the projects in this book were carefully chosen, and I've described all the fabrics so you have a feel for how they affect the design and its wear-ability. Of course you may substitute other yarns for any of the projects, and I have made suggestions. However, for successful fit, take care to obtain the same gauge as the original pattern.

Warm weather yarns are a little fussier in care and handling than many resilient wools and animal fibers used for warmer garments, but they are well worth the effort for their coolness, drape and texture. Be sure to read the labels for any yarn that you consider, and take care to follow the specific instructions for cleaning and use of heat, cautions for either ironing and/or steaming.

1. Get the correct gauge, knitting a good-sized swatch — at least 6" (15 cm) by 6" (15 cm). Remind yourself that the little time it takes is worth your investment in yarn.

2. Since many summer yarn choices, often plant fibers, do not have the "springiness" of wool or other animal fibers, you may find that it is valuable to do two things to insure accurate gauge and reliable fit in the final sweater. First, if you sense that a yarn might stretch, work your initial swatch on a smaller needle. Then, even though this might sound silly, carry your swatch in your bag, handle it on and off for a few days to see if it stretches. Check your gauge more accurately after this small effort. If the gauge stays the same, then you can be assured that the garment too will not stretch.

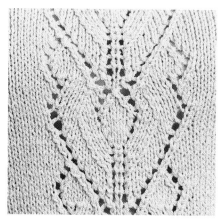  

3. Block your swatch, if necessary. Not all yarns worked in synthetic and plant fibers can be successfully steamed. So, gauge swatches — and final sweaters — may need to be handled more carefully than those knitted with wool or animal fibers. To even out irregularities in the fabric, wet blocking is usually fine. Or you can lay a damp towel over pieces until the swatch or pieces are dry. Strong fibers like cotton and linen can take heat, but do still take care when steaming or pressing to retain the texture of the knitting, and not flatten it. Again, be sure to study the label of your yarn for proper care advice.

4. If you are unsure about a yarn substitution for any project in this book, consult an experienced knitter or an expert in a yarn store. It is fun to be adventurous and try a new yarn/ fiber that might be totally new to you. Research new yarns, see what other knitters have to say about them and compare to your needs, likes and dislikes. Online sources can give you a sense of what a yarn is like before you try it.

5. Lastly, (and although it goes against the theme of this book!) many of these designs can be translated to another cooler season by working in a winter-season yarn. For a garment less close-to-the-body than you would wear in the summer, perhaps you might make it one size larger.

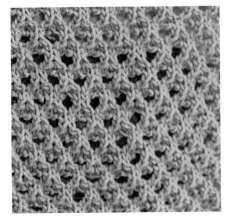

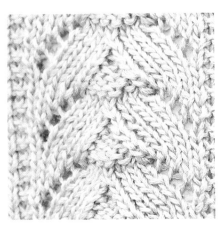

Be-Ribbed & Be-Ribboned
CARDIGAN

▰▰▰▱ INTERMEDIATE

SIZES
To fit sizes Small {Medium-Large-Extra Large}
Sample in size Medium.

MEASUREMENTS
Finished bust at underarm: 32{36-40-44}"/81.5{91.5-101.5-112} cm
Length to back neck, before finishing: 21^1/$_2${22-22^1/$_2$-23}"/54.5{56-57-58.5} cm
Sleeve width at upper arm: 10{10-12^1/$_2$-15^1/$_2$}"/25.5{25.5-32-39.5} cm

Size Note: Instructions are written for size Small with sizes Medium, Large and X-Large in braces { }. Instructions will be easier to read if you circle all the numbers pertaining to your size. If only one number is given, it applies to all sizes.

✳   ✳   ✳   ✳   ✳   ✳   ✳   ✳   ✳   ✳   ✳   ✳   ✳   ✳   ✳   ✳   ✳   ✳

In JASMINE yarn from Louisa Harding
This is a dressy, fitted cardigan that is knitted in a soft blend of cotton, bamboo and silk, and has a glint of metallic gold. The ribbing shapes the waistline of the garment without decreases. The little patterns at the lower edge and the yoke are easy to work. The wide neckline keeps the sweater cool.

For detail, I added some orange-tinted mother-of-pearl buttons etched with flowers. After adding these buttons, the knitted cord I had planned for below the bust seemed dull, and I picked out a luscious silk ribbon to weave through the eyelets.

This is a sweater for a party! But in different coloration, perhaps with stripes, and with a yarn tie, it could take on a more casual, even nautical look.

The elbow-length sleeve can be folded up for a sportier look, or could be shortened. For a tiny cap sleeve effect, cast on as for the regular sleeve and work just for an inch or so. In the same vein, the sleeve could also be lengthened to full length — the ribbed pattern, without shaping, would make a pretty flared look.

Instructions begin on page 10.

MATERIALS

LOUISA HARDING
"Jasmine" (LIGHT 3)
(48% Cotton, 39% Bamboo, 10% Silk, 3% Polyester; 50 grams/107 yards)
Color #5 (Custard): 8{9-11-13} balls
Straight knitting needles, sizes 5 (3.75 mm) **and** 6 (4 mm) **or** size needed to obtain gauge
Cable needle (cn)
Stitch markers
1" (25 mm) Buttons - 8
1½" wide (38 mm) Silk ribbon - 48" (122 cm)

GAUGE

Over Cable Panel using larger needles: 23 sts and 26 rows = 4" (10 cm)
Take time to save time, check your gauge.

Techniques used:
• YO **(Figs. 2a-d, page 122)**
• K2 tog **(Fig. 4, page 123)**
• P2 tog **(Fig. 5, page 123)**
• SSK **(Figs. 7a-c, page 124)**
• M1 **(Figs. 3a & b, page 123)**

STITCH GUIDE

Right Twist (RT): K2 tog leaving sts on LH needle, then knit first st again; slip both sts from needle.

Left Twist (LT): Skip 1 st and knit into back of 2nd st, then knit in front of the skipped st; slip both sts from needle.

PATTERN STITCHES
CABLE PANEL: 13-st Panel

Rows 1, 3 and 5 (RS): P4, K1, (P1, K1) 2 times, P4.
Rows 2, 4 and 6 (WS): K4, P1, (K1, P1) 2 times, K4.
Rows 7, 9 and 11: P4, K1, YO, K2 tog, YO, K2 tog, P4.
Rows 8, 10 and 12: K4, P1, (K1, P1) 2 times, K4.
Row 13: P2, slip 2 sts to cn and hold in back, K2, K1, P1 from cn, K1, slip 2 sts to cn and hold in front, P1, K1, K2 from cn, P2.
Row 14: K2, P3, K1, P1, K1, P3, K2.
Row 15: P1, slip 1 st to cn and hold in back, K2, P1 from cn, K1, (P1, K1) 2 times, slip 2 sts to cn and hold in front, P1, K2 from cn, P1.
Row 16: K1, P2, K1, (P1, K1) 3 times, P2, K1.
Row 17: P1, K2, P1, (K1, P1) 3 times, K2, P1.
Row 18: K1, P2, K1, (P1, K1) 3 times, P2, K1.
Rep Rows 1-18 for Cable Panel.

RIBBED PANEL: 4-st Panel

Rows 1 and 3 (RS): K1, P2, K1.
Row 5: RT, LT.
Rows 2, 4 and 6 (WS): P1, K2, P1.
Rep Rows 1-6 for Ribbed Panel.

SLEEVE RIB: Multiple of 15 sts plus 11

Row 1 (RS): * P3, K1, (P1, K1) 2 times, P3, K1, P2, K1; rep from * across to last 11 sts, P3, K1, (P1, K1) 2 times, P3.
Row 2 (WS): K3, P1, (K1, P1) 2 times, K3, * P1, K2, P1, K3, P1, (K1, P1) 2 times, K3; rep from * across.
Rep Row 1 and 2 for Rib.

STOCKINETTE STITCH (St st): Any number of sts
Knit on RS, purl on WS.

REVERSE STOCKINETTE STITCH (Rev St st): Any number of sts
Purl on RS, knit on WS.

BACK

With larger needles, cast on 96{108-120-132} sts.

Establish Patterns for sizes as follows, placing markers between Panels.

Small: K2 (edge sts), P5 (keep in Rev St st), work 4-st Ribbed Panel, P1 (keep in Rev St st), work 4-st Ribbed Panel, [work 13-st Cable Panel, work 4-st Ribbed Panel] 4 times, P1 (keep in Rev St st), work 4-st Ribbed Panel, P5 (keep in Rev St st), K2 (edge sts).

Medium: K2 (edge sts), P3 (keep in Rev St st), work 13-st Cable Panel, [work 4-st Ribbed Panel, work 13-st Cable Panel] 5 times, P3 (keep in Rev St st), K2 (edge sts).

Large: K2 (edge sts), P5 (keep in Rev St st), work 4-st Ribbed Panel, [work 13-st Cable Panel, work 4-st Ribbed Panel] 6 times, P5 (keep in Rev St st), K2 (edge sts).

X-Large: K2 (edge sts), [P1 (keep in Rev St st), work 4-st Ribbed Panel] 3 times, [work 13-st Cable Panel, work 4-st Ribbed Panel] 6 times, [P1 (keep in Rev St st), work 4-st Ribbed Panel] 2 times, P1 (keep in Rev St st), K2 (edge sts).

ALL Sizes
Keeping 2 edge sts each side in St st, work in Patterns as established until 18 rows of Cable Panel have been worked 3 times.

Next Row (RS): Change to Rib Pattern and decrease as follows: Over each 4-st Ribbed section work K1, P2, K1. Over each 13-st Cable section work P1, P2 tog, P1, (K1, P1) 3 times, P2 tog, P1. Work all remaining sts as established — 88{96-108-120} sts.

Work in ribs as established (knit the knit sts and purl the purl sts as they appear) until piece measures 12" (30.5 cm), end RS.

Place eyelets:
To work a single eyelet, over 2 sts: K2 tog, YO.
Mark next row for placement of 10{14-14-14} eyelets, spaced as desired.

Instructions continued on page 12.

Eyelet Row (WS): Work in pattern as established, working 10{14-14-14} eyelets as marked.

Next Row (RS): Work in pattern as established.

Continue in ribs as established until piece measures 16" (40.5 cm), end RS.

Increase Row (WS): Work 16{5-11-17} sts as established, * K1, M1, K2, work 5 sts as established, K1, M1, K2, work 4 sts as established; rep from * across to last 12{16-7-13} sts, [K1, M1, K2, work 5 sts as established, K1, M1, K2] 0{1-0-0} time(s) *(see Zeros, page 121)*, work last 12{5-7-13} sts as established — 96{108-120-132} sts.

Change back to Cable and Ribbed Patterns as for beginning of Back. Work as established until piece measures 17" (43 cm), end WS.

Raglan Armhole Shaping (RS): Work as follows for size:

Small (RS): Bind off 4 sts at beginning of next 2 rows.
Next (decrease) Row (RS): K1, SSK, work in patterns to last 3 sts, K2 tog, K1.
Rep decrease row [alternately every 4th and 2nd row] 3 times, then every RS row 4 times — 66 sts.

Medium (RS): Bind off 4 sts at beginning of next 2 rows.
Next (decrease) Row (RS): K1, SSK, work in patterns to last 3 sts, K2 tog, K1.

Rep decrease row [alternately every 4th and 2nd row] 1 time, then every RS row 11 times — 72 sts.

Large (RS): Bind off 5 sts at beginning of next 2 rows, then 2 sts at beginning of next 2 rows.
Next (decrease) Row (RS): K1, SSK, work in patterns to last 3 sts, K2 tog, K1.
Rep decrease row every RS row 14 times — 76 sts.

X-Large (RS): Bind off 6 sts at beginning of next 2 rows, then 2 sts at beginning of next 8 rows.
Next (decrease) Row (RS): K1, SSK, work in patterns to last 3 sts, K2 tog, K1.
Rep decrease row every RS row 13 times — 76 sts.

ALL Sizes
Back Neck Shaping (RS): Mark center 28{34-38-38} sts.

Next Row (RS): K1, SSK, work to marker; join second ball of yarn and bind off center 28{34-38-38} sts, work to last 3 sts, K2 tog, K1.

Working both sides at once, bind off at each Neck edge 5 sts 3 times AND AT THE SAME TIME continue decreases at each side 3 times more.

LEFT FRONT

With larger needles, cast on 48{54-60-66} sts.

Establish Patterns for sizes as follows:

Small: K2 (edge sts), P5 (keep in Rev St st), work 4-st Ribbed Panel, P1 (keep in Rev St st), [work 4-st Ribbed Panel, work 13-st Cable Panel] 2 times, K2 (edge sts).

Medium: K2 (edge sts), P3 (keep in Rev St st), work 13-st Cable Panel, [work 4-st Ribbed Panel, work 13-st Cable Panel] 2 times, K2 (edge sts).

Large: K2 (edge sts), P5 (keep in Rev St st), [work 4-st Ribbed Panel, work 13-st Cable Panel] 3 times, K2 (edge sts).

X-Large: K2 (edge sts), [P1 (keep in Rev St st), work 4-st Ribbed Panel] 3 times, work 13-st Cable Panel, [work 4-st Ribbed Panel, work 13-st Cable Panel] 2 times, K2 (edge sts).

ALL Sizes
Keeping 2 edge sts each side in St st, work in Patterns as established until 18 rows of Cable Panel have been worked 3 times.

Next Row (RS): Change to Rib Pattern and decrease as follows: Over each 4-st Ribbed section work K1, P2, K1.
Over each 13-st Cable section work P1, P2 tog, P1, (K1, P1) 3 times, P2 tog, P1.

Work all remaining sts as established — 44{48-54-60} sts.

Work in ribs as established (knit the knit sts and purl the purl sts as they appear) until piece measures 12" (30.5 cm), end RS.

Place eyelets:
To work a single eyelet over 2 sts: K2 tog, YO.
Mark next row for placement of 4{6-6-6} eyelets, spaced as desired.

Eyelet Row (WS): Work in pattern as established, working 4{6-6-6} eyelets as marked.

Next Row (RS): Work in pattern as established.

Continue in ribs as established until piece measures 16" (40.5 cm), end RS.

Increase Row (WS):
P2, * K1, M1, K2, work 5 sts as established, K1, M1, K2, work 4 sts as established; rep from * across to last 12{16-7-13} sts, [K1, M1, K2, work 5 sts as established, K1, M1, K2] 0{1-0-0} time(s), work last 12{5-7-13} sts as established — 48{54-60-66} sts.

Change back to Cable and Ribbed Patterns as for beginning of Left Front. Work as established until piece measures 17" (43 cm), end WS.

Raglan Armhole Shaping (RS): Work as follows for size:

Small (RS): Bind off 4 sts at the beginning of the row.

Next (decrease) Row (RS):
K1, SSK, work to end.
Rep decrease row [alternately every 4th and 2nd row] 3 times, then every RS row 2 times — 35 sts.

Medium (RS): Bind off 4 sts at the beginning of the row.
Next (decrease) Row (RS):
K1, SSK, work in patterns to end.
Rep decrease row [alternately every 4th and 2nd row] 1 time, then every RS row 9 times — 38 sts.

Large (RS): Bind off 5 sts at the beginning of the row, then 2 sts at beginning of next RS row.
Next (decrease) Row (RS):
K1, SSK, work in patterns to end.
Rep decrease row every RS row 12 times — 40 sts.

X-Large (RS): Bind off 6 sts at the beginning of the row, then 2 sts at beginning of next 4 RS rows.
Next (decrease) Row (RS):
K1, SSK, work in patterns to end.
Rep decrease row every RS row 11 times — 40 sts.

ALL Sizes
Front Neck Shaping (WS):
Bind off 14{17-19-19} sts, work to end.

Continue to decrease at beginning of RS rows 3 times more AND AT THE SAME TIME bind off at beginning of WS rows 6 sts 3 times.

RIGHT FRONT
With larger needles, cast on 48{54-60-66} sts.

Establish Patterns for sizes as follows:

Small: K2 (edge sts), [work 13-st Cable Panel, work 4-st Ribbed Panel] 2 times, P1 (keep in Rev St st), work 4-st Ribbed Panel, P5 (keep in Rev St st), K2 (edge sts).

Medium: K2 (edge sts), work 13-st Cable Panel, [work 4-st Ribbed Panel, work 13-st Cable Panel] 2 times, P3 (keep in Rev St st), K2 (edge sts).

Large: K2 (edge sts), [work 13-st Cable Panel, work 4-st Ribbed Panel] 3 times, P5 (keep in Rev St st), K2 (edge sts).

X-Large: K2 (edge sts), [work 13-st Cable Panel, work 4-st Ribbed Panel] 3 times, [P1 (keep in Rev St st), work 4-st Ribbed Panel] 2 times, P1 (keep in Rev St st), K2 (edge sts).

ALL Sizes
Complete as for Left Front, reversing all shaping and placement of eyelets.

RIGHT SLEEVE
With larger needles, cast on 60{60-75-90} sts.

Instructions continued on page 14.

Establish Patterns (RS):
K2 (edge sts), work in Sleeve Rib Pattern over 56{56-71-86} sts, end K2 (edge sts).

Keeping 2 edge sts each side in St st, work even until piece measures 8" (20.5 cm), end WS.

Raglan Cap Shaping (RS):
Work as follows for size:

Small (RS): Bind off 4 sts at the beginning of the next 2 rows.
Next (decrease) Row (RS):
K1, SSK, work in patterns to last 3 sts, K2 tog, K1.
At Beginning of Rows: Rep decrease [alternately every 4th and 2nd row] 1 time, then every RS row 11 times AND at the end of rows [alternately every 4th and 2nd row] 4 times, then every RS row 2 times — 27 sts.

Medium (RS): Bind off 4 sts at the beginning of the next 2 rows.
Next (decrease) Row (RS):
K1, SSK, work in patterns to last 3 sts, K2 tog, K1.
At Beginning of Rows: Rep decrease [alternately every 4th row and 2nd row] 2 times, then every RS row 9 times AND at the end of rows [alternately every 4th and 2nd row] 5 times — 27 sts.

Large (RS): Bind off 5 sts at the beginning of the next 2 rows.
Next Row (RS): Bind off 2 sts, work in patterns to last 3 sts, K2 tog, K1.
Rep last row every RS row 2 times.

Next (decrease) Row (RS):
K1, SSK, work in patterns to last 3 sts, K2 tog, K1.
Rep last row every RS row 13 times — 28 sts.

X-Large (RS): Bind off 6 sts at the beginning of the next 2 rows, then 2 sts at beginning of next 8 rows.
Next Row (RS): Bind off 2 sts, work in patterns to last 3 sts, K2 tog, K1.
Rep last row every RS row 2 times.
Next (decrease) Row (RS):
K1, SSK, work in patterns to last 3 sts, K2 tog, K1.
Rep last row every RS row 11 times — 29 sts.

ALL Sizes
Top of Cap Shaping (RS):
Bind off at beginning of RS rows, 6 sts 4{4-3-2} times, then 0{0-7-7} sts 0{0-1-2} time(s) AND AT THE SAME TIME continue to decrease 1 st at the end of rows 3 times.

LEFT SLEEVE

Work same as Right Sleeve, except reverse shaping at top of Cap by beginning shaping 1 row later, on WS row.

FINISHING

Sew Fronts to Sleeves to Back at Raglan seam lines *(Fig. 16, page 127)*. There should be 2 sts in St st at each raglan seam line.

Sew side and Sleeve seams.

Neckline Trim: With smaller needles and RS facing, pick up 34{36-38-38} sts along Right Front edge *(Figs. 15a & b, page 127)*, pick up 2 sts at raglan seam, pick up 25 sts along top of Sleeve, pick up 2 sts at raglan seam, pick up 65{69-71-71} sts along Back Neck edge, pick up 2 sts at raglan seam, pick up 25 sts along top of Sleeve, pick up 2 sts at raglan seam, pick up 34{36-38-38} sts along Left Front edge — 191{199-205-205} sts.

Establish Patterns (WS):
P2, (K1, P1) 15{16-17-17} times, K2, P2 (at raglan seam), K2, P1, (K1, P1) 10 times, K2, P2 (at raglan seam), K2, P1, (K1, P1) 30{32-33-33} times, K2, P2 (at raglan seam), K2, P1, (K1, P1) 10 times, K2, P2 (at raglan seam), K2, (P1, K1) 15{16-17-17} times, end P2.

Row 1 (RS): Knit the knit sts and purl the purl sts AND AT THE SAME TIME, work RT over each 2-st raglan seam.

Row 2: Work WS row as established.

Next (decrease) Row 3 (RS):
(Work as established to 4 sts before the 2-st raglan seam, K2 tog, P2, K2, P2, SSK) 4 times, work as established to end — 183{191-197-197} sts.

Row 4: Work WS as established.

Rep the last 4 rows once more —
175{183-189-189} sts.

Bind off on next row AND
AT THE SAME TIME work
decreases as established at
raglan seams (Row 3) and work
RT before binding off RT Cable
at seams.

Left Front Band: With smaller
needles and RS facing, pick up
116{119-122-125} sts along
entire Front edge.

Knit 7 rows.

Bind off all sts in knit.

**Right Front Buttonhole
Band:** With smaller needles and
RS facing, pick up
116{119-122-125} sts along
entire Front edge.

Knit WS row.

Next (buttonhole) Row (RS):
K 12{15-18-21}, * make 3-st
buttonhole (by binding off
3 sts and casting on 3 sts while
working bind off row), K 11; rep
from * across to last 6 sts, end
* make 3-st buttonhole, knit to
end — 8 buttonholes.

Complete band as for Left Front
Band.

Sew buttons opposite
buttonholes.

Thread ribbon through eyelets.❋

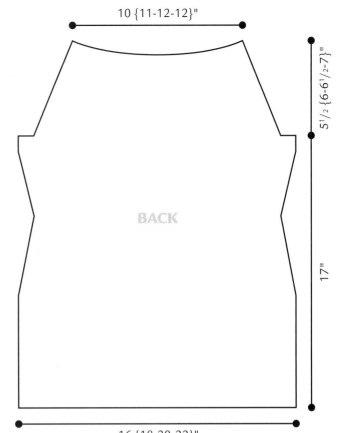

10 {11-12-12}"

BACK

5¹/₂ {6-6¹/₂-7}"

17"

16 {18-20-22}"

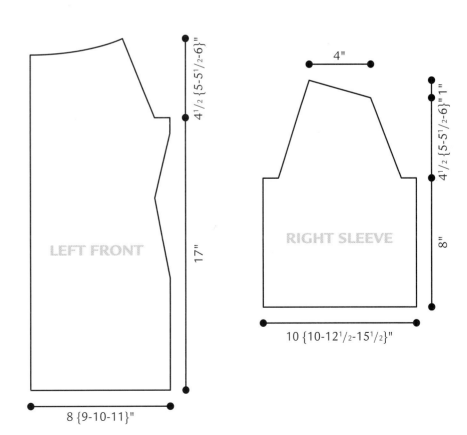

LEFT FRONT

4¹/₂ {5-5¹/₂-6}"

17"

8 {9-10-11}"

RIGHT SLEEVE

4"

4¹/₂ {5-5¹/₂-6}" 1"

8"

10 {10-12¹/₂-15¹/₂}"

Claudette
CARDI

◖■■■◗ INTERMEDIATE

SIZES
To fit sizes Small {Medium-Large-Extra Large}
Sample in size Small.

MEASUREMENTS
Finished bust at underarm: 36{40-44-48}"/91.5{101.5-112-122} cm
Length to mid shoulder, approximately 2" (5 cm) above outer shoulder:
21{21¹/₂-22-22¹/₂}"/53.5{54.5-56-57} cm

Size Note: Instructions are written for size Small with sizes Medium, Large
and X-Large in braces { }. Instructions will be easier to read if you circle all the
numbers pertaining to your size. If only one number is given, it applies to all sizes.

❋ ❋ ❋ ❋ ❋ ❋ ❋ ❋ ❋ ❋ ❋ ❋ ❋ ❋ ❋ ❋ ❋ ❋ ❋

In SKINNY COTTON yarn from Blue Sky Alpaca
Luckily for me, the idea for this sweater emerged quickly with many little details coming together
to form the final design. I had the little wooden toggles on my desk, and I had been staring at
a skein of the most beautifully colored cotton for a week or so! And I had just watched a movie
from the 30's with Claudette Colbert, where she wore a top that had interesting diagonal lines so
characteristic of that period. I had also recently been playing around with a lace pattern I never
used before, one that slanted on the bias when knit. Something that pulled everything together was
the desire to make a fitted sweater that had a vintage feel, yet still looked modern.

There you have it — I just sketched a few things with all of the above in mind, and it all came
together. And what pleased me to no end was that this sweater is a lot of fun to knit, as well as
having a distinctive look. The best part for me was that the naturally occurring diagonal direction
of the lace at the shoulders creates the shaping that makes the sweater's V-neck and cap sleeve.

Almost any summer yarn will work in this little cardi. A drapier yarn might make the fabric and the
points of the lace at the shoulders a little softer.

Instructions begin on page 18.

MATERIALS

BLUE SKY ALPACA
"Skinny Cotton"
(100% Organically
Grown Cotton;
65 grams/150 yards)
Color #317 (Coral):
7{7-8-9} hanks
Straight knitting needles,
sizes 6 (4 mm) **and**
7 (4.5 mm) **or** sizes
needed to obtain gauge
Cable needle (cn)
Stitch markers
³/₈" wide x ³/₄" long
(10 cm x 19 cm) Small
wooden toggle buttons
Yarn needle

GAUGE

Over Textured Pattern
using larger needles:
22 sts and 30 rows =
4" (10 cm)
Over 13-st Cable Panel
measures approximately
2" (5 cm) wide
Over Lace Bias patterns
using smaller needles:
approximately 18 sts
and 24 rows = 4" (10 cm)
Take time to save time,
check your gauge.

Techniques used:

• K1 tbl *(Fig. 12, page 126)*
• YO *(Figs. 2a-d, page 122)*
• K2 tog *(Fig. 4, page 123)*
• SSK *(Figs. 7a-c, page 124)*
• M1 *(Figs. 3a & b, page 123)*
• Slip 1 as if to **knit**, K2 tog, PSSO *(Figs. 9a & b, page 125)*

PATTERN STITCHES
STOCKINETTE STITCH

(St st): Any number of sts
Knit RS rows, purl WS rows.

TEXTURED PATTERN:

Multiple of 4 sts plus 2
Row 1 (RS): Knit across.
Row 2: Purl across.
Row 3: K2, * P2, K2; rep from * across.
Row 4: P2, * K2, P2; rep from * across.
Rep Rows 1-4 for Textured Pattern.

CABLE PANEL: 13-sts Panel

Preparation Row (RS): P2, K1 tbl, P1, K5, P1, K1 tbl, P2.

Row 1 and all WS rows: K2, P1, K1, P5, K1, P1, K2.
Rows 2, 4 and 6: P2, K1 tbl, P1, K1 tbl, YO, slip 1, K2 tog, PSSO, YO, K1 tbl, P1, K1 tbl, P2.
Row 8: P2, slip 2 sts to cn and hold in back, K1, then slip the purl st from cn back to LH needle and purl it, then K1 from cn, K1 tbl, K1, K1 tbl, slip 2 sts to cn and hold in front, K1, then slip the purl st from cn to LH needle and purl it, then K1 from cn, P2.
Row 10: P2, K1 tbl, P1, YO, SSK, K1, K2 tog, YO, P1, K1 tbl, P2.
Rep Rows 1-10 for Cable Panel.

RIGHT LEANING BIAS LACE:

(even number of sts)
Row 1 (RS): K1, * YO, K2 tog; rep from * across to last st, K1.
Row 2 (WS): Purl across.
Rep Rows 1 and 2 for Right Leaning Bias Lace.

LEFT LEANING BIAS LACE:

even number of sts)
Row 1 (RS): K1, * SSK, YO; rep from * across to last st, K1.
Row 2 (WS): Purl across.
Rep Rows 1 and 2 for Left Leaning Bias Lace.

Note 1: The Lace yoke sections for each piece are picked up along upper edges of Back and Front. Cables are continued from lower sections, without being bound off.

Note 2: For extensions at lower armholes, to cast on at beginning and/or end of rows, use backward loops *(Fig. 1, page 121)* OR use the cable cast-on method at the beginning of rows as follows:
With beginning of row facing where sts are to be cast on, insert RH needle between 1st and 2nd sts, pull through a loop *(Fig. A)* and place loop on LH needle *(Fig. B)*; * then insert RH needle between 1st st (newly made loop) on LH needle and next st, pull through another loop and place loop on LH needle; rep from * until desired number of sts are cast on AND AT THE SAME TIME, after pulling through last loop and before placing it on the LH needle, bring yarn from back to front, in between it, and to separate it, from the last loop on LH needle.

Fig. A   **Fig. B**

BACK

Lower Section: Cast on 104{112-128-136} sts.

Establish Patterns (RS):
K2 (edge sts), work Row 1 of Textured Pattern over 34{38-46-50} sts, place marker (PM) *(see Markers, page 121)*, work Preparation Row of 13-st Cable Panel, PM, work Row 1 of Textured Pattern over center 6 sts, PM, work Preparation Row of 13-st Cable Panel, PM, work Row 1 of Textured Pattern over 34{38-46-50} sts, K2 (edge sts).

Keeping 2 edge sts each side in St st, work even in patterns for 15 more rows.

Waist (decrease) Row (RS):
K1, SSK, work as established to last 3 sts, K2 tog, K1.

Keeping in patterns, rep decrease row every 6th row 3 more times — 96{104-120-128} sts.

Work even until piece measures 7" (18 cm), end WS.

Waist (increase) Row (RS):
K2, M1, work as established to last 2 sts, M1, K2.

Keeping in patterns, rep increase row every 6th row 3 more times — 104{112-128-136} sts.

Work even until piece measures 12" (30.5 cm), end WS.

Instructions continued on page 20.

Extension at Armhole (RS): Keeping in patterns as established and working cast-on sts in Textured pattern, cast on 3 sts at the beginning of the next 8 rows — 128{136-152-160} sts.

Work even in patterns until piece measures 15{15^1/$_2$-16-16^1/$_2$}"/ 38{39.5-40.5-42} cm, end RS.

End Lower Back Section (WS): Bind off 48{52-60-64} sts, work 13-st Cable Panel as established, P2, bind off center 2 sts, P1, work 13-st Cable Panel as established, bind off remaining 48{52-60-64} sts.

Back Lace Yoke Sections:
Note: Both sections of the Back Yoke will be worked at the same time with separate balls of yarn. For the neatest look, pick up the first st into the first st below, and the last st before cable into the st below that is right next to the cable; the rest of the sts evenly space between.

Next Row (RS):
With RS facing, pick up 37{41-45-49} sts evenly to Cable *(Figs. 15a & b, page 127)*, PM, work 13-st Cable Panel as established, end K2 (edge sts); join a second ball of yarn and, on next side, K2 (edge sts), work 13-st Cable Panel as established, PM, pick up 37{41-45-49} sts evenly to end — 52{56-60-64} sts each side.

Next Row (WS):
P 37{41-45-49} sts to Cable, slip marker, continue 13-st Cable Panel as established, P2; on second side, P2, continue 13-st Cable Panel as established, slip marker, P 37{41-45-49} sts.

Establish Patterns (RS):
K1 (edge st), work Row 1 of Right Leaning Bias Lace over 36{40-44-48} sts, slip marker, continue 13-st Cable Panel as established, end K2 (edge sts); on second side, K2 (edge sts), continue 13-st Cable Panel as established, slip marker, work Row 1 of Left Leaning Bias Lace over 36{40-44-48} sts, K1 (edge st).

Working both sides at the same time with separate balls of yarn, work even in patterns as established until yoke sections measure 4" (10 cm), end WS.

Shoulder Shaping (RS):
Keeping in pattern, loosely bind off from each shoulder edge, 6 sts 6{4-2-0} times *(see Zeros, page 121)*, then 8 sts 2{4-6-8} times.

LEFT FRONT

Lower Section: Cast on 51{55-63-67} sts.

Establish Patterns (RS):
K2 (edge sts), work Row 1 of Textured Pattern over 34{38-46-50} sts, PM, work Preparation Row of 13-st Cable Panel, PM, K2 (edge sts).

Keeping 2 edge sts each side in St st, work even in patterns for 15 more rows.

Waist (decrease) Row (RS):
K1, SSK, work as established to end.

Keeping in patterns, rep decrease row every 6th row 3 more times — 47{51-59-63} sts.

Work even until piece measures 7" (18 cm), end WS.

Waist (increase) Row (RS):
K2 (edge sts), M1, work as established to end.

Keeping in patterns, rep increase row every 8th row 3 more times — 51{55-63-67} sts.

Work even until piece measures 12" (30.5 cm), end WS.

Extension at Armhole:
Keeping in patterns and working cast-on sts into Textured Pattern, cast on 3 sts at the beginning of the next 4 RS rows — 63{67-75-79} sts.

Work even until piece measures 15{15^1/$_2$-16-16^1/$_2$}"/ 38{39.5-40.5-42} cm, end RS.

End Lower Front Section (WS): P2, work 13-st Cable Panel as established, bind off remaining 48{52-60-64} sts.

Lace Yoke Section (RS):
With RS facing, pick up 37{41-45-49} sts evenly to Cable, PM, work 13-st Cable Panel as established, K2 (edge sts) — 52{56-60-64} sts.

Next Row (WS): P2, continue 13-st Cable Panel as established, slip marker, P 37{41-45-49} sts.

Establish Patterns (RS): K1 (edge st), work Row 1 of Right Leaning Bias Lace over 36{40-44-48} sts, slip marker, continue 13-st Cable Panel as established, K2 (edge sts).

Work even in pattern until Yoke section measures 4" (10 cm), end WS.

Shoulder Shaping (RS): Keeping in pattern, loosely bind off on RS rows, 6 sts 6{4-2-0} times, then 8 sts 2{4-6-8} times.

RIGHT FRONT

Work same as for Left Front, reversing all shaping and pattern placement and using Left Leaning Bias Lace.

FINISHING

Sew Fronts to Back at sides including extensions at underarms *(Fig. 16, page 127)*.

Sew Lace Sections at shoulders together where they meet.

Left Front Button Band: With RS facing, pick up 78{81-84-87} sts along Left Front edge below Lace section.

Knit 5 rows.

Bind off all sts in knit.

Right Front Buttonhole Band: With RS facing, pick up 78{81-84-87} sts along Right Front edge below Lace Section.

Next (buttonhole) Row (WS): K1, * K2 tog, YO, SSK, K4; rep from * until there are 10 YO's, knit across.

Next RS Row: Knit, work (K1, P1) into each YO of previous row.

Complete as for Left Band.

Sew buttons opposite buttonholes. ✳

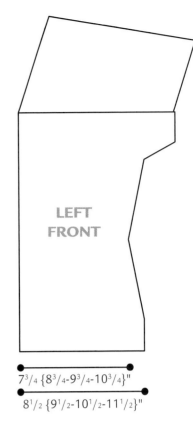

LEFT FRONT

7³/₄ {8³/₄-9³/₄-10³/₄}"

8¹/₂ {9¹/₂-10¹/₂-11¹/₂}"

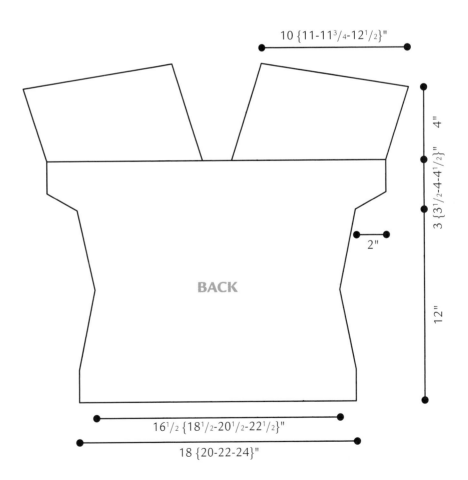

BACK

10 {11-11³/₄-12¹/₂}"

4"

3 {3¹/₂-4-4¹/₂}"

2"

12"

16¹/₂ {18¹/₂-20¹/₂-22¹/₂}"

18 {20-22-24}"

Community Garden
SUMMER BAGS

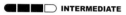 **INTERMEDIATE**

FINISHED MEASUREMENTS
Large Natural bag with Knitted handles:
   approximately 18" x 18" (45.5 cm x 45.5 cm)
Two Colored bag with Buttoned handle:
   approximately 14" x 14" (35.5 cm x 35.5 cm)

✳   ✳   ✳   ✳   ✳   ✳   ✳   ✳   ✳   ✳   ✳   ✳   ✳   ✳   ✳   ✳   ✳   ✳

VERSION #1: "Natural" bag in SPROUT from Classic Elite
VERSION #2: "Colored" bag in SECOND TIME COTTON from Knit One Crochet Too

I had been looking for a way to use this pattern — it is an old-fashioned coverlet square. Here I updated it in new yarns. I have varied the "medallion" design, as well as the simple strap, in two different ways.

For the larger bag, I chose a soft nubby "green" yarn — a 100% organically-grown cotton. The soft texture gives the bag a lazy droopiness. The strap is simply tied on each side — the knot becomes an interesting detail!

The sturdy smaller bag is worked in a finer gauge yarn that is strong and firm, a blend of recycled cotton and acrylic. I chose some decorative buttons this time, to add detail to the bag.

Use this simple medallion concept with your own yarn choices, details, and colors! A very heavy cotton would make an even larger version — or how about joining 4 medallions on each side of a bag? Any number of straps could be devised: a braid of narrow bands, or a wide cable, or even one made of sewn fabric, to match a fabric lining.

MATERIALS
LARGE NATURAL BAG
CLASSIC ELITE "Sprout"
(100% Organic Cotton;
100 grams/109 yards)
  Color #4316 (Natural):
  4 hanks
Double-pointed needles
  (set of five), size 10
  (6 mm) **or** size needed to
  obtain gauge
Straight knitting needles,
  size 9 (5.5 mm)
  36" (91.5 cm) Circular
  needle, size 10 (6 mm)
Stitch markers

COLORED BAG
KNIT ONE CROCHET TOO "Second Time Cotton"
(75% Recycled Cotton,
25% Acrylic;
100 grams/180 yards)
  Color A: #841 (Coral):
  2 skeins
  Color B: #847 (Khaki):
  2 skeins
Double-pointed needles
  (set of five), size 8 (5 mm)
  or size needed to
  obtain gauge
Straight knitting needles,
  size 8 (5 mm)
24" (61 cm) Circular
  needle, size 8
1" (25 mm) Button (or
  desired size) - 2
Stitch markers

Instructions begin on page 24.

23

GAUGE

Over Lace Square using "Sprout" and size 10 needles: approximately 11 sts = 4" (10 cm)
Over Lace Square using "Second Time Cotton" and size 8 needles: approximately 14 sts = 4" (10 cm)
Take time to save time, check your gauge.

Techniques used:
- YO **(Fig. 2a, page 122)**
- K2 tog **(Fig. 4, page 123)**
- SSK **(Figs. 7a-c, page 124)**

LACE SQUARE

Note: Each line of instruction should be repeated 4 times, once on each needle. Change to circular needle if necessary, placing markers between sections.

Cast on 8 sts. Distribute evenly on 4 needles, knit with 5th needle.
Rnd 1 and all odd numbered rounds: Knit.
Rnd 2: K1, YO, K1.
Rnd 4: (K1, YO) 2 times, K1.
Rnd 6: K1, YO, K3, YO, K1.
Rnd 8: K1, YO, K5, YO, K1.
Rnd 10: K1, YO, K7, YO, K1.
Rnd 12: K1, YO, K9, YO, K1.
Rnd 14: K1, YO, K 11, YO, K1.
Rnd 16: K1, YO, K 13, YO, K1.
Rnd 18: K1, YO, K 15, YO, K1.
Rnd 20: (K1, YO) 2 times, K5, SSK, K1, K2 tog, K5, (YO, K1) 2 times.
Rnd 22: (K1, YO) 2 times, SSK, YO, K4, SSK, K1, K2 tog, K4, YO, K2 tog, (YO, K1) 2 times.
Rnd 24: (K1, YO) 2 times, (SSK, YO) 2 times, K3, SSK, K1, K2 tog, K3, (YO, K2 tog) 2 times, (YO, K1) 2 times.
Rnd 26: (K1, YO) 2 times, (SSK, YO) 3 times, K2, SSK, K1, K2 tog, K2, (YO, K2 tog) 3 times, (YO, K1) 2 times.
Rnd 28: (K1, YO) 2 times, (SSK, YO) 4 times, K1, SSK, K1, K2 tog, K1, (YO, K2 tog) 4 times, (YO, K1) 2 times.
Rnd 30: (K1, YO) 2 times, (SSK, YO) 5 times, SSK, K1, K2 tog, (YO, K2 tog) 5 times, (YO, K1) 2 times.
Rnd 32: (K1, YO) 2 times, (SSK, YO) 6 times, slip 1, K2 tog, PSSO, (YO, K2 tog) 6 times, (YO, K1) 2 times.
Rnd 34: (K1, YO) 2 times, (SSK, YO) 6 times, SSK, K1, K2 tog, (YO, K2 tog) 6 times, (YO, K1) 2 times.
Rnd 36: (K1, YO) 2 times, (SSK, YO) 7 times, slip 1, K2 tog, PSSO, (YO, K2 tog) 7 times, (YO, K1) 2 times.
Rnd 38: (K1, YO) 2 times, (SSK, YO) 7 times, SSK, K1, K2 tog, (YO, K2 tog) 7 times, (YO, K1) 2 times.
Rnd 40: (K1, YO) 2 times, (SSK, YO) 8 times, slip 1, K2 tog, PSSO, (YO, K2 tog) 8 times, (YO, K1) 2 times.
Rnd 41: Knit — 41 sts each side.

LARGE NATURAL BAG (Make 2 squares)

With "Sprout" and size 10 dpns, cast on 8 sts.

Work Rnds 1-41 of Lace Square.

Garter Border: Again, each line of instruction should be repeated 4 times, once on each needle.

Rnd 1: K1, YO, work to last st of needle, YO, K1.

Rnd 2: Purl.

Rep the last 2 rnds until there are 49 sts on each needle, end with a purl rnd — 49 sts each side.
Leave sts of first square on circular needle for joining.

Join Squares: With WS of squares facing each other, bind off the 2 squares together on 3 sides as follows: Holding the needles for both squares tog, K2 tog (one st from each square), knit next 2 sts from each needle tog, then pass the first st over second st to bind off.
Continue to bind off sts until 3 sides of the squares are joined.

Opening Edges: Bind off the remaining two edges separately for bag opening.

Loops: (Make 2)
With size 10 needle, cast on 14 sts. Purl 1 row. Bind off. Fold in half and sew one to each upper corner, forming a loop.

Handle: With size 9 needle, cast on 120 sts.

Knit 8 rows.

Bind off all sts in knit.

Thread each end of handle through a loop on the bag and tie in a knot, then reinforce the knot by sewing invisibly through it to hold in place.

COLORED BAG

First Square: With "Second Time Cotton" Color A, and size 8 dpns, cast on 8 sts.

Work Rnds 1-41 of Lace Square. Change to B.

Garter Border: Again, each line of instruction should be repeated 4 times, once on each needle.

Rnd 1: K1, YO, work to last st of needle, YO, K1.

Rnd 2: Purl.

Rep the last 2 rnds until there are 49 sts each needle, end with a purl rnd — 49 sts each side. Leave sts on circular needle for joining.

Second Square: Work as for First Square, reversing colors.

Join as for Large Bag.

Strap: With B and size 8 needles, cast on 75 sts.

Knit 2 rows. Change to A, knit 2 rows. Change to B, knit 4 rows. Change to A, knit 4 rows. Change to B, knit 2 rows. Change to A, knit 2 rows.

Bind off in knit to end of Strap, do not cut yarn, then pick up 1 st for each garter st ridge along end of strap — 8 sts. Knit 1 row. Bind off all sts in knit.

On other end of Strap, with B, pick up 8 sts. Knit 1 row. Bind off all sts in knit.

Center ends of Strap to each side of opening, and sew button to hold in place, through all layers. ✳

25

Frida Lace PULLOVER

 **INTERMEDIATE**

SIZES
To fit sizes Small {Medium-Large-Extra Large}
Sample in size Medium.

MEASUREMENTS
Finished bust at underarm: 34{38-42-46}"/86.5{96.5-106.5-117} cm
Length to shoulder: 20{20-20^1/$_2$-21}"/51{51-52-53.5} cm
Sleeve width at upper arm: 14{14^1/$_2$-15^1/$_2$-16^1/$_2$}"/35.5{37-39.5-42} cm

Size Note: Instructions are written for size Small with sizes Medium, Large
and X-Large in braces { }. Instructions will be easier to read if you circle all the
numbers pertaining to your size. If only one number is given, it applies to all sizes.

✳   ✳   ✳   ✳   ✳   ✳   ✳   ✳   ✳   ✳   ✳   ✳   ✳   ✳   ✳   ✳   ✳   ✳   ✳

In CLICHÉ yarn from JCA/Artful yarns
I wanted this sweater to be an updated look for traditional lace patterns, in a simple, easy to knit
shape. And it's a nod to Mexican artist Frida Kahlo who wore wonderful lace-trimmed blouses.

I used the "wrong side" of the lace patterns in this sweater for a fresh look. Traditionally, lace
patterns present their smoother stockinette stitch side as the "right side," but I have noticed — and
you should too! — that the opposite side, rougher and more textured, often is more captivating!

This yarn — a mix of cotton, linen, and a little acrylic — knits a fabric soft, drapey, and cool to the
touch. For a little extra air on a hot day, I left the side of the lace borders open.

Instructions begin on page 28.

MATERIALS

JCA/ARTFUL YARNS
"Clichè" **MEDIUM 4**
(55% Cotton, 30% Linen,
15% Acrylic;
50 grams/112 yards)
Color #5 (Easy as Pie):
6{7-8-8} balls
Straight knitting needles,
sizes 6 (4 mm) **and**
7 (4.5 mm) **or** sizes
needed to obtain gauge
One straight fine knitting
needle, any size 1-4

GAUGE

Over St st and Wide Lace
Pattern using larger needles:
20 sts and 26 rows =
4" (10 cm)
Take time to save time,
check your gauge.

Techniques used:

• YO **(Fig. 2a, page 122)**
• K2 tog **(Fig. 4, page 123)**
• SSK **(Figs. 7a-c, page 124)**
• Slip 1 as if to **knit**, K2 tog,
  PSSO **(Figs. 9a & b,
  page 125)**

PATTERN STITCHES
REVERSE STOCKINETTE STITCH (Rev St st): Any number of sts
Purl RS rows, knit WS rows.

STOCKINETTE STITCH (St st): Any number of sts
Knit RS rows, purl WS rows.

ZAGGED LACE BORDER: (Begins with 20 sts, st count varies from row to row)
With larger needles, cast on
20 sts and knit 1 row.
Row 1 (WS): Slip 1 (as if to
purl), K3, (YO, K2 tog) 7 times,
YO, K2.
Rows 2, 4, 6 and 8 (RS): Knit
across.
Row 3: Slip 1, K6, (YO, K2 tog)
6 times, YO, K2.
Row 5: Slip 1, K9, (YO, K2 tog)
5 times, YO, K2.
Row 7: Slip 1, K 12, (YO,
K2 tog) 4 times, YO, K2.
Row 9: Slip 1, K 23.
Row 10: Bind off 4 sts, K 19.
Rep Rows 1-10 for Zagged Lace
Border.

WIDE LACE PATTERN:
Multiple of 10 sts plus 3
Row 1 (WS): K1, * YO, SSK,
K8; rep from *, end YO, SSK,
K7, K2 tog, YO, K1.
**Rows 2, 4, 6, 8, 10, 12, 14,
16, 18, 20 and 22:** Purl across.
Row 3: K1, * K1, YO, SSK, K5,
K2 tog, YO; rep from * across to
last 2 sts, K2.
Row 5: K1, * K2, YO, SSK,
K3, K2 tog, YO, K1; rep from *
across to last 2 sts, K2.
Row 7: K1, * (YO, SSK, K1) 2
times, K2 tog, YO, K2; rep from
*, end (YO, SSK, K1) 2 times,
K2 tog, YO, K1, K2 tog, YO, K1.
Row 9: K1, * K1, YO, SSK, K1,
YO, slip 1, K2 tog, PSSO, YO,
K1, K2 tog, YO; rep from *
across to last 2 sts, K2.
Row 11: Rep Row 5.
Row 13: Rep Row 7.
Row 15: Rep Row 9.
Row 17: Rep Row 5.
Row 19: K1, * K3, YO, SSK,
K1, K2 tog, YO, K2; rep from *
across to last 2 sts, K2.
Row 21: K1, * K4, YO, slip 1,
K2 tog, PSSO, YO, K3; rep from
* across to last 2 sts, K2.
Row 23: K1, P1, * SSK, K2, YO,
K1, YO, K2, K2 tog, P1; rep from
* across to last st, K1.
**Rows 24, 26, 28, 30, 32, 34
and 36 (RS):** P1, K1, * P9, K1;
rep from * across to last st, P1.
**Rows 25, 27, 29, 31, 33 and
35 (WS):** Rep Row 23.
Rows 37-58: Rep Rows 1-22.

Instructions continued on page 30.

BACK

Note: Zagged Border is worked first, then the sts for the upper back are picked up along the straight edge.

With larger needles, cast on 20 sts and knit 1 row.

Work Zagged Lace Border until 160{180-200-220} rows are complete — 16{18-20-22} full reps.

Bind off all sts.

Pick up for Upper Back: With RS facing, beginning at left edge using smaller fine needle, slip needle into 80{90-100-110} purl sts (every other row) along straight edge of Zagged Border, plus 1 extra at cast on edge — 81{91-101-111} sts.

Continuing with larger needles, purl RS row and increase 6 sts evenly spaced *(see Increasing or Decreasing Evenly Across A Row, page 123)* — 87{97-107-117} sts.

Next Row (WS): P2 (edge sts), work 83{93-103-113} sts in Rev St st, P2 (edge sts).

Keeping 2 edge sts each side in St st, work as established for 1" (2.5 cm) above Zagged Border, end RS.

Next (eyelet) Row (WS): P2, K1{0-1-1} *(see Zeros, page 121)*, * K2 tog, YO, K1; rep from * across to last 3{2-2-3} sts, K1{0-0-1}, P2.

Purl RS row.

Continue in Rev St st until piece measures 2¹/₂" (6.5 cm) above Zagged Border, end RS.

Next Row (WS): P2, work Row 1 of Wide Lace Pattern over 83{93-103-113} sts, P2.

Work even until 58 rows of Wide Lace Pattern are complete.

Knit WS row.

Continue in Rev St st until Back measures approx 1" (2.5 cm) above Wide Lace Pattern, end with a RS row.

Rep eyelet row.

Work in Rev St st until piece measures 3{3-3¹/₂-4}"/ 7.5{7.5-9-10} cm above Wide Lace Pattern, end with a WS row.

Shoulder and Back Neck Shaping (RS): Mark center 39{39-39-41} sts.

Next Row (RS): Bind off 5{7-8-9} sts, work to center marked sts; join a second ball of yarn and bind off center 39{39-39-41} sts, work to end.

Working both sides at once with separate balls of yarn, bind off 5{7-8-9} sts from the next 3 shoulder edges, then 4{5-8-10} sts from the next 2 shoulder edges AND AT THE SAME TIME bind off 5 sts from each Neck edge twice.

FRONT

Work same as for Back until piece measures 2{2-2¹/₂-3}"/ 5{5-6.5-7.5} cm above Wide Lace Pattern, end WS.

Front Neck Shaping (RS): Mark center 39{39-39-41} sts.

Next Row (RS): Work to center marked sts; join a second ball of yarn and bind off center 39{39-39-41} sts, work to end.

Working both sides at once with separate balls of yarn, bind off 2 sts at each Neck edge 5 times AND AT THE SAME TIME, when Front measures same as Back to shoulder end WS.

Shoulder Shaping (RS): Bind off from each shoulder edge 5{7-8-9} sts twice then 4{6-8-10} sts once.

SLEEVES

Note: Zagged Border is worked first, then the sts for upper sleeve are picked up along the straight edge.

With larger needles, cast on 20 sts and knit 1 row.

Work Zagged Lace Border until 130{140-150-160} rows are complete — 13{14-15-16} full reps.

Bind off all sts.

Pick up for Upper Sleeve:
With RS facing, beginning at left edge using smaller fine needle, slip needle into 65{70-75-80} purl sts (every other row) along straight edge of Zagged Border, plus 1 extra at cast on edge — 66{71-76-81} sts.

Continuing with larger needles, purl RS row and increase 5{3-4-5} sts evenly spaced — 71{74-80-86} sts.

Next Row (WS): P2 (edge sts), work 67{70-76-82} sts in Rev St st, P2 (edge sts).

Next (eyelet) Row (WS): P2 (edge sts), K1, * K2 tog, YO, K1; rep from * across to last 2 sts, P2 (edge sts).

Purl RS row.

Continue in Rev St st until piece measures 1½" (4 cm) above Zagged Border, end with a RS row.

Bind off all sts in knit.

FINISHING

Sew Front to Back at shoulders.

Place markers 7{7¼-7¾-8¼}"/ 18{18.5-19.5-21} cm down from shoulders on Front and Back.
Sew Sleeve tops between markers.

Sew side and Sleeve seams above Zagged Border **(Fig. 16, page 127)**, leaving borders open at sides.

Front Neck Finishing: With RS facing and smaller needles, pick up 70{70-70-72} sts evenly along Front Neck edge **(Figs. 15a & b, page 127)**.

P1 row, K1 row, P1 row.

Bind off all sts in knit.

Back Neck Finishing: With RS facing and smaller needles, pick up 63{63-63-65} sts evenly along Back Neck edge.

P1 row, K1 row, P1 row.

Bind off all sts in knit.

Weave in ends, allowing trim to roll to RS. ✳

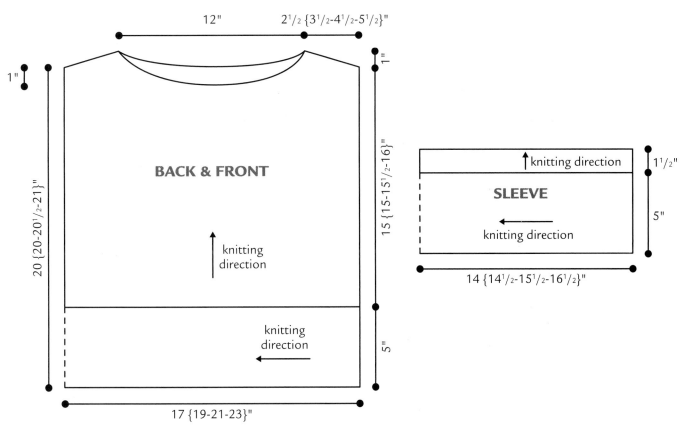

Fuji Summer KIMONO

◖◖◖◗ INTERMEDIATE

SIZES
To fit sizes Small {Medium-Large-Extra Large}
Sample in size Small.

MEASUREMENTS
Finished bust at underarm, fronts free: 41{46-51-56}"/104{117-129.5-142} cm
Length to shoulder: 27{27^1/$_2$-28-28^1/$_2$}"/68.5{70-71-72.5} cm
Sleeve width at upper arm: 18{20^1/$_2$-23-25^1/$_2$}"/45.5{52-58.5-65} cm

Size Note: Instructions are written for size Small with sizes Medium, Large
and X-Large in braces { }. Instructions will be easier to read if you circle all the
numbers pertaining to your size. If only one number is given, it applies to all sizes.

✳   ✳   ✳   ✳   ✳   ✳   ✳   ✳   ✳   ✳   ✳   ✳   ✳   ✳   ✳   ✳   ✳

In COTTON STRIA yarn from Manos Del Uruguay
A woman of Japanese heritage in my neighborhood has a bank of beautiful columbine plants along
the sidewalk. They bloom in early summer every year. She told me once that she gathered the seeds
on Mount Fuji and brought them home to plant them in her garden.

I look forward to those complex blooms of varying colors, and the varied greens of the foliage, too.
Here I combine the notion of those plants of Fuji origin with one of my favorite ethnic garments, the
Japanese kimono. Then to break the theme — I chose a hand-dyed cotton from Uruguay!

A hint: Deep color is often held brilliantly in soft cottons, so make that something you consider when
searching for brightly colored yarns.

Instructions begin on page 34.

MATERIALS

MANOS DEL URUGUAY
"Cotton Stria"
(100% Pure Peruvian
Kettle-Dyed Cotton;
50 grams/116 yards)
   A: #203 (Olive):
      5{5-6-7} hanks
   B: #221 (Flax):
      2{2-2-3} hanks
   C: #205 (Melon):
      2{2-3-3} hanks
   D: #201 (Violet):
      3{3-3-3} hanks
   E: #204 (Pistachio):
      3{4-4-4} hanks
Straight knitting needles,
   sizes 6 (4 mm) **and**
   7 (4.5 mm) **or** size
   needed to obtain gauge
24" (61 cm) Circular
   knitting needle, size 6
   (4 mm)
3/4" (19 mm) Button
Smooth cotton yarn for
   seaming

GAUGE

Over Reverse Basket Weave
St using larger needles:
19 sts and 27 rows =
4" (10 cm)
Take time to save time,
check your gauge.

PATTERN STITCHES

STOCKINETTE STITCH
(St st): Any number of sts
Knit RS rows, purl WS rows.

REVERSE BASKET WEAVE STITCH (Rev Basket Weave St): Multiple of 6 sts plus 2

Row 1 (RS): Purl across.
Rows 2 and 4: K2, * P4, K2; rep from * across.
Rows 3 and 5: P2, * K4, P2; rep from * across.
Row 6: Knit across.
Row 7: Purl across.
Rows 8 and 10: P3, * K2, P4; rep from * across to last 5 sts, K2, P3.
Rows 9 and 11: K3, * P2, K4; rep from * across to last 5 sts, P2, K3.
Row 12: Knit across.
Rep Rows 1-12 for Rev Basket Weave St.

COLOR SEQUENCE

*12 rows B, 12 rows A,
6 rows D, 12 rows E, 6 rows A,
** 12 rows C, 12 rows A,
6 rows B, 12 rows D, 6 rows A,
*** 12 rows E, 12 rows A,
6 rows C, 12 rows B, 6 rows A,
**** 12 rows D, 12 rows A,
6 rows E, 12 rows D, 6 rows C.
Rep from * for Color Sequence.

BACK

With smaller needles and E, cast on 94{104-114-124} sts. K2 rows.

Change to A and knit every row until piece measures 2" (5 cm), end RS.

Purl WS row increasing 8{10-12-14} sts evenly spaced **(see Increasing or Decreasing Evenly Across A Row, page 123)** — 102{114-126-138} sts.

Change to larger needles and begin Color Sequence at *.

Next Row (RS): K2 (edge sts), place marker (PM) **(see Markers, page 121)**, work Row 1 of Rev Basket Weave St over 98{110-122-134} sts, PM, K2 (edge sts).

Keeping 2 edge sts each side in St st, work as established until piece measures 27{27¹/₂-28-28¹/₂}"/ 68.5{70-71-72.5} cm, end WS.

Back Neck and Shoulder Shaping (RS): Mark center 22{24-28-32} sts. Bind off 10{12-13-14} sts, work to marker; join a second ball of yarn and bind off center 22{24-28-32} sts, work to end.

Working both sides at the same time, continue to bind off 10{12-13-14} sts at the beginning of the next 5{3-5-3} rows, then 0{11-0-15} sts at the beginning of the next 2 rows **(see Zeros, page 121)** AND AT THE SAME TIME, bind off at each Neck edge 5 sts twice.

Instructions continued on page 36.

LEFT FRONT

With smaller needles and C, cast on 43{48-53-58} sts. K2 rows.

Change to A and knit every row until piece measures 2" (5 cm), end RS.

Purl WS row, increasing 4{5-6-7} sts evenly spaced — 47{53-59-65} sts.

Change to larger needles and begin Color Sequence at **, then rep from *.

Next Row (RS): K2 (edge sts), PM, work Row 1 of Rev Basket Weave St over 44{50-56-62} sts, PM, K1 (Front edge st).

Keeping edge sts each side in St st, continue as established until piece measures 14" (35.5 cm), end WS.

V-Neck Shaping (decrease) Row (RS): Work across to last 2 sts, K2 tog.

WS Rows: P1, work as established to end.

Rep decrease row every 4th row 16{17-19-21} times more — 30{35-39-43} sts.

Work even until Front measures same as Back to shoulder, end with a WS row.

Shoulder Shaping (RS): Bind off 10{12-13-14} sts at the beginning of the next 3{2-3-2} shoulder edges, then 0{11-0-15} sts at the beginning of the next 1 shoulder edge.

RIGHT FRONT

Work same as for Left Front, reversing all shaping and placement of patterns, EXCEPT cast on with D, and begin Color Sequence with Band at ***, then rep from *.

LEFT SLEEVE

With smaller needles and E, cast on 83{94-104-115} sts. K2 rows.

Change to A and knit every row until piece measures 2" (5 cm), end RS.

Purl WS row increasing 7{8-10-11} sts evenly spaced — 90{102-114-126} sts.

Change to larger needles and begin Color Sequence at *.

Next Row (RS): K2 (edge sts), PM, work Row 1 of Rev Basket Weave St over 86{98-110-122} sts, PM, K2 (edge sts).

Keeping 2 edge sts each side in St st, continue as established until Sleeve measures 10" (25.5 cm), end WS.

Bind off all sts in knit.

RIGHT SLEEVE

With smaller needles and C, cast on 83{94-104-115} sts. K2 rows.

Change to A and knit every row until piece measures 2" (5 cm), end RS.

Purl WS row increasing 7{8-10-11} sts evenly spaced — 90{102-114-126} sts.

Change to larger needles and begin Color Sequence at ****, then rep from *.

Next Row (RS): K2 (edge sts), PM, work Row 1 of Rev Basket Weave St over 86{98-110-122} sts, PM, K2 (edge sts).

Keeping 2 edge sts each side in St st, continue as established until Sleeve measures 10" (25.5 cm), end WS.

Bind off all sts in knit.

FINISHING

Sew Fronts to Back at shoulders.

Place markers 9{10¼-11½-12¾}"/ 23{26-29-32.5} cm down from shoulders on Front and Back. Sew Sleeve tops between markers.

Sew side and Sleeve seams *(Fig. 16, page 127)*.

Lower Left Front Trim: With larger needles, RS facing and E, beginning at V-Neck Shaping, pick up 68 sts along Left Front edge to lower edge *(Figs. 15a & b, page 127)*.

Knit 11 rows AND AT THE SAME TIME, decrease 1 st at beginning of every RS row. Change to D and knit 2 rows, continue decreasing on RS row.

Bind off all sts in knit.

Lower Right Front Trim: With larger needles, RS facing and E, beginning at lower edge, pick up 68 sts along Right Front edge to beginning of V-Neck Shaping.

Knit 11 rows AND AT THE SAME TIME, decrease 1 st at end of every RS row. Change to C and knit 2 rows, continue decreasing on RS row.

Bind off all sts in knit.

Left Front V-Neck Trim: Mark center 4 sts at Back Neck. With larger needles, RS facing and A, beginning at right of 4 center sts, pick up 21{22-24-26} sts to shoulder, then 72{74-76-78} sts along V-Neck to lower Left Front Trim, then 7 sts along top of trim — 100{103-107-111} sts.

Knit 11 rows AND AT THE SAME TIME, increase 1 st at each end of every RS row. Continuing increases, change to D and knit 2 rows, then change to C and knit 2 rows.

Bind off all sts in knit.

Right Front V-Neck Trim: With larger needles, RS facing and B, beginning at top of lower Right Front Trim, pick up 7 sts along top of trim, 72{74-76-78} sts along V-Neck edge, then 21{22-24-26} sts to left of center 4 sts — 100{103-107-111} sts.

Knit 11 rows AND AT THE SAME TIME, increase 1 st at each end of every RS row. Continuing increases, change to C and knit 2 rows, then change to D and knit 2 rows.

Bind off all sts in knit but do not cut strand, pick up 1 st for every ridge along side of band, knit 1 row. Bind off all sts in knit.

Overlap the point of this center back band over the left front band and secure with button sewn through both layers.

Steam edges lightly, but do not press. ✳

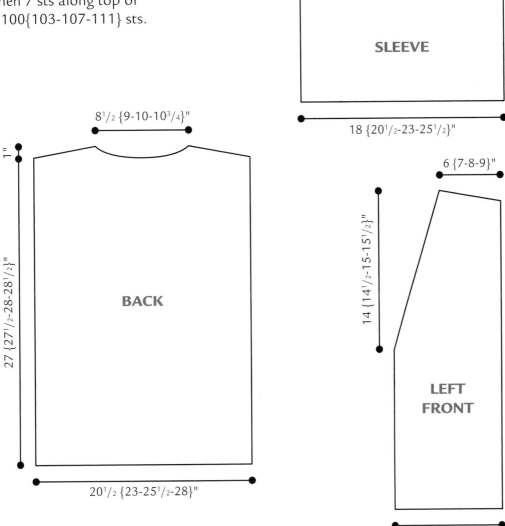

SLEEVE 10"

18 {20¹/₂-23-25¹/₂}"

8¹/₂ {9-10-10³/₄}"

1"

27 {27¹/₂-28-28¹/₂}"

BACK

20¹/₂ {23-25¹/₂-28}"

6 {7-8-9}"

14 {14¹/₂-15-15¹/₂}"

LEFT FRONT

9¹/₄ {10¹/₂-11¹/₂-13}"

Honeycomb & Leaf
SHAWL

◖■■■▢ **INTERMEDIATE**

SIZES
One size

MEASUREMENTS
Width at top: 52" (132 cm)
Length at longest point: 27" (68.5 cm)

＊　＊　＊　＊　＊　＊　＊　＊　＊　＊　＊　＊　＊　＊　＊　＊　＊　＊

In BERGEREINE yarn from Bergere De France
I intended this shawl to be a simple allover honeycomb, but at the wider end it cried out for detail, so I added some leaves. The eyelets are interesting made as double yarn-overs, wrapping the yarn twice around the needle, making each hole larger and more textured than eyelets made with a single yarn-over.

Often a wool yarn that is mixed with cotton has the springiness of the animal fiber with a softer feel. The blend I used for this shawl is crisp, with a hard twist, and not at all fuzzy — a good choice for warm weather as it sits on the skin without adhering to it!

But any yarn at all would work for this shawl — for a luxurious heavy drape, use a silk or rayon. For a crisper, even drier feel try a linen or linen blend. The softer new fibers — like soy or bamboo — have a pretty sheen and also drape nicely.

Instructions begin on page 40.

MATERIALS

BERGERE DE FRANCE "Bergereine"
(50% Cotton, 50% Wool; 50 grams/103 yards)
Color #21770 (Salmon): 6 skeins
24" (61 cm) Circular knitting needle, size 8 (5 mm) **or** size needed to obtain gauge
Stitch markers

GAUGE

Over Honeycomb Pattern:
17 sts and 26 rows = 4" (10 cm)
Take time to save time, check your gauge.

Techniques used:

- YO *(Figs. 2a-d, page 122)*
- M1 *(Figs. 3a & b, page 123)*
- K2 tog *(Fig. 4, page 123)*
- P2 tog *(Fig. 5, page 123)*
- P2 tog tbl *(Fig. 6, page 124)*
- SSK *(Figs. 7a-c, page 124)*

PATTERN STITCHES

STOCKINETTE STITCH

(St st): Any number of sts
Knit RS rows, purl WS rows.

GARTER STITCH

(Garter St): Any number of sts
Knit every row.

HONEYCOMB EYELET PATTERN: Multiple of 4 sts plus 2

Row 1: K1, * K2 tog, YO twice, SSK; rep from * across to last st, K1.
Row 2: P2, * (P1, K1) into double YO of previous row, P2; rep from * across.
Row 3: Knit across.
Row 4: Purl across.
Rep Rows 1-4 for Honeycomb Eyelet Pattern.

LEAF BORDER: (23 sts)

Row 1 (RS): K8, K2 tog, YO, K1, P1, K1, YO, SSK, K8.
Row 2: P7, P2 tog tbl, P2, YO, K1, YO, P2, P2 tog, P7.
Row 3: K6, K2 tog, K1, YO, K2, P1, K2, YO, K1, SSK, K6.
Row 4: P5, P2 tog tbl, P3, YO, P1, K1, P1, YO, P3, P2 tog, P5.
Row 5: K4, K2 tog, K2, YO, K3, P1, K3, YO, K2, SSK, K4.
Row 6: P3, P2 tog tbl, P4, YO, P2, K1, P2, YO, P4, P2 tog, P3.
Row 7: K2, K2 tog, K3, YO, K4, P1, K4, YO, K3, SSK, K2.
Row 8: P1, P2 tog tbl, P5, YO, P3, K1, P3, YO, P5, P2 tog, P1.
Row 9: K2 tog, K4, YO, K5, P1, K5, YO, K4, SSK.
Row 10: P 11, K1, P 11.
Row 11: K 11, P1, K 11.
Row 12: P 11, K1, P 11.

SHAWL

Note: Working back and forth on a circular needle, the shawl is started at the lowest point, the Honeycomb Eyelet motifs are worked into pattern as sts are increased and the shawl ends with the Leaf Border. Shorter needles may be used to start, change to longer circular needle when required.

Cast on 10 sts.

Knit 5 rows.

Next Row (WS): K2 (edge sts), P6, K2 (edge sts).

Establish Pattern Row 1 (RS): K2, M1, work Row 1 of Honeycomb Eyelet Pattern across to last 2 sts, M1, K2.

Row 2 (WS): K2, P1, work Row 2 of Honeycomb Eyelet Pattern across to last 3 sts, P1, K2.

Row 3: K2, M1, work Row 3 of Honeycomb Eyelet Pattern across to last 2 sts, M1, K2.

Row 4: K2, work Row 4 of Honeycomb Eyelet Pattern across to last 2 sts, K2.

Rep last 4 rows, working increases into Honeycomb Eyelet Pattern when possible, until there are 190 sts, ending with Row 3.

Next Row (WS): K2, purl across to last 2 sts increasing 21 sts evenly spaced *(see Increasing or Decreasing Evenly Across a Row, page 123)*, K2 — 211 sts.

Next Row (RS): K2, M1, place marker (PM) *(see Markers, page 121)*, work 9 repeats of Leaf Border over 207 sts, PM, M1, K2.

Keeping Garter St edge sts and working increases into St st, work until 12 rows of Leaf Border Pattern are complete, end WS.

Knit next row, continue to increase 1 st at beginning and end of row and, decrease 1 st at center of each of the 9 leaf motifs.

Work 8 rows in Garter St and continue to increase at beginning and end of each RS row.

Bind off all sts in knit.

Steam lightly. ✳

Narragansett Breeze
TWIN SET

◖■■■▭ INTERMEDIATE

CARDIGAN AND HALTER SIZES
To fit sizes Extra Small {Small-Medium-Large}
Sample in size Small.

MEASUREMENTS
Cardigan:
Finished bust at underarm: 32{36-40-44}"/81.5{91.5-101.5-112} cm
Length, from back neck, below neckline edging: $17^1/2${18-$18^1/2$-19}"/44.5{45.5-47-48.5} cm
Sleeve width at upper arm: 11{12-$13^1/2$-15}"/28{30.5-34.5-38} cm
Halter:
Finished bust at underarm: 31{35-39-43}"/78.5{89-99-109} cm
Length, from back neck includes casing (does not include drawstring):
$15^1/2${16-$16^1/2$-17}"/39.5{40.5-42-43} cm

Size Note: Instructions are written for size X-Small with sizes Small, Medium and Large in braces { }. Instructions will be easier to read if you circle all the numbers pertaining to your size. If only one number is given, it applies to all sizes.

✳   ✳   ✳   ✳   ✳   ✳   ✳   ✳   ✳   ✳   ✳   ✳   ✳   ✳   ✳   ✳   ✳

In HEMPATHY yarn from ELSEBETH LAVOLD
Cardigan & Halter
Knitted in a light and airy yarn, this twin set is perfect for the hottest of days. This finer gauge yarn features hemp mixed with cotton and modal, and creates a featherweight fabric with a crisp quality.

Both the halter and cardigan are short and cool, and either of them could be lengthened without changes to the pattern. The shell pattern is easy to knit, and the knit ridges give detail without effort.

For substitutions, I would suggest only light yarns for these pieces. This fabric has a very dry-feeling, matte-finish — a linen or linen blend might duplicate that feeling. Perhaps you could like a shinier or more opalescent version? If so, try a bamboo or rayon — or blends — with a sheen.

Buttons are always a fascination for me, and they add detail. Here I used small vintage toggles which I found online for the cardi. I sewed tiny wood button to the ends of the knitted halter cord. Look for just the right button to tickle your fancy — there are so many to choose from online, both vintage and new.

Instructions begin on page 44.

MATERIALS

ELSEBETH LAVOLD **LIGHT 3**
  "Hempathy"
(34% Hemp, 41% Cotton, 25% Modal;
50 grams/154 yards)
Color #32 (Fluorite Blue)
  Cardigan:
    5{6-7-7} skeins
  Halter: 4{4-5-5} skeins
Straight knitting needles, sizes 5 (3.75 mm) **and** 6 (4 mm) **or** size needed to obtain gauge
24" (61 cm) Circular needle, size 5 (3.75 mm)
Stitch markers
3/4" (19 mm) Toggle buttons - 3
  (for cardigan)
1/2" (12 mm) Wood buttons - 2
  (optional for halter)

GAUGE

Over Garter Stripe Pattern using larger needles:
22 sts and 32 rows = 4" (10 cm)
Take time to save time, check your gauge.

Techniques used:

- YO **(Fig. 2a, page 122)**
- K2 tog **(Fig. 4, page 123)**
- SSK **(Figs. 7a-c, page 124)**
- K4 tog **(Fig. 11, page 125)**

PATTERN STITCHES
STOCKINETTE STITCH
(St st): Any number of sts
Knit RS rows, purl WS rows.

REVERSE STOCKINETTE STITCH (Rev St st): Any number of sts
Purl RS rows, knit WS rows.

GARTER STRIPE PATTERN: Any number of sts
Rows 1, 3, 5 and 7 (RS): Knit across.
Rows 2, 4 and 6: Purl across.
Row 8: Knit across.
Rep Rows 1-8 for Garter Stripe Pattern.

SHELL PATTERN: Multiple of 9 sts plus 3 (St count varies from row to row)
S4K = slip 4 sts knitwise, one at a time, then insert LH needle from the left into the front of the 4 sts (now on the RH needle), and K4 tog this way.

Row 1 (RS): K2, * YO, K8, YO, K1; rep from * to last st, K1.
Row 2: K3, * P8, K3; rep from * across.
Row 3: K3, * YO, K8, YO, K3; rep from * across.
Row 4: K4, * P8, K5; rep from * across, end last rep K4.
Row 5: K4, * YO, K8, YO, K5; rep from * across, end last rep K4.
Row 6: K5, * P8, K7; rep from * across, end last rep K5.
Row 7: K5, * S4K, K4 tog, K7; rep from * across, end last rep K5.
Row 8: Knit across.
Rep Row 1-8 for Shell Pattern.

CARDIGAN
BACK

With larger needles, cast on 88{98-110-122} sts.

Establish Patterns (RS):
Work Row 1 of Garter Stripe Pattern over 11{16-22-28} sts, place marker (PM) **(see Markers, page 121)**, work Row 1 of Shell Pattern over 66 sts, PM, work Row 1 of Garter Stripe Pattern over remaining 11{16-22-28} sts.

Work even in patterns as established until 3 reps of Shell Pattern (24 rows) are complete.

Establish Patterns (RS):
Work Row 1 of Garter Stripe Pattern over 20{25-31-37} sts, PM, work Row 1 of Shell Pattern over 48 sts, PM, work Row 1 of Garter Stripe Pattern over remaining 20{25-31-37} sts.

Work even in patterns as established until 3 more reps of Shell Pattern are complete.

Establish Patterns (RS):
Work Row 1 of Garter Stripe Pattern over 29{34-40-46} sts, PM, work Row 1 of Shell Pattern over 30 sts, PM, work Row 1 of Garter Stripe Pattern over remaining 29{34-40-46} sts.

Work even in patterns as established until 3 more reps of Shell Pattern are complete.

Establish Patterns (RS):
Work Row 1 of Garter Stripe Pattern over 38{43-49-55} sts, PM, work Row 1 of Shell Pattern over 12 sts, PM, work Row 1 of Garter Stripe Pattern over remaining 38{43-49-55} sts.

Work even in patterns as established until 3 more reps of Shell Pattern are complete.

Piece measures approximately 12" (30.5 cm). Change to all Garter Stripe Pattern for remainder of piece.

Raglan Armhole Shaping (RS): Bind off 5 sts at the beginning of the next 2 rows.

Next (decrease) Row (RS):
K1, SSK, work as established to last 3 sts, K2 tog, K1.

Work decrease row as follows for size.
X-Small: Rep decrease row every 4th row 5 times, then every 6th row 3 times — 60 sts. Bind off on next RS row.

Small: Rep decrease row every 4th row 11 times — 64 sts. Bind off on next RS row.

Medium: Rep decrease row [alternately every 4th, then every 2nd row] 8 times — 66 sts. Bind off on next RS row.

Large: Rep decrease row [alternately ever 4th, then every 2nd row] 5 times, then every 2nd row 10 times — 70 sts. Bind off on next RS row.

Instructions continued on page 46.

LEFT FRONT

With larger needles, cast on 41{46-52-58} sts.

Establish Patterns (RS):
Work Row 1 of Garter Stripe Pattern over 11{16-22-28} sts, PM, work Row 1 of Shell Pattern over remaining 30 sts.

Work even in patterns as established until 3 reps of Shell Pattern (24 rows) are complete.

Establish Patterns (RS):
Work Row 1 of Garter Stripe Pattern over 20{25-31-37} sts, PM, work Row 1 of Shell Pattern over remaining 21 sts.

Work even in patterns as established until 3 more reps of Shell Pattern are complete.

Establish Patterns (RS):
Work Row 1 of Garter Stripe Pattern over 29{34-40-46} sts, PM, work Row 1 of Shell Pattern over remaining 12 sts.

Work even in patterns as established until 3 more reps of Shell Pattern are complete.

Change to all Garter Stripe Pattern for remainder of piece and work until piece measures same as Back to Armhole, end WS.

Raglan Armhole Shaping (RS): Bind off 5 sts at the beginning of the next RS row.

Work WS row.

Next (decrease) Row (RS):
K1, SSK, work as established to end.

Work decrease row as follow for size.
X-Small: Rep decrease row every 4th row 5 times, then every 6th row 2 times — 28 sts.
Bind off on next RS row.

Small: Rep decrease row every 4th row 9 times, then every 2nd row once — 30 sts.
Bind off on next RS row.

Medium: Rep decrease row [alternately every 4th, then every 2nd row] 7 times — 32 sts.
Bind off on next RS row.

Large: Rep decrease row [alternately every 4th, then every 2nd row] 4 times, then every 2nd row 10 times — 34 sts.
Bind off on next RS row.

RIGHT FRONT

Work same as for Left Front, reversing pattern placement and shaping.

RIGHT SLEEVE

With larger needles, cast on 57{66-75-84} sts.

Work in Shell Pattern for 16 rows.

Change to Garter Stripe Pattern and work for 8 rows.

Raglan Armhole Shaping (RS): Bind off 5 sts at the beginning of the next 2 rows.

Work 2 rows even.

Next (decrease) Row (RS):
K1, SSK, work as established to last 3 sts, K2 tog, K1.

Work decrease row as follows for size.
X-Small: Rep decrease row every 6th row once, then every 4th row 6 times — 31 sts.

Small: Rep decrease row [alternately every 2nd row, then every 4th row] 6 times — 30 sts.

Medium: Rep decrease row [alternately every 2nd row, then every 4th row] 4 times, then every 2nd row 8 times — 31 sts.

Large: Rep decrease row every 2nd row 21 times — 30 sts.

ALL Sizes
Top of Cap Shaping (RS):
Bind off 7 sts, work to end.

Work WS row.

Next Row (RS): Bind off 7 sts, work to last 3 sts, K2 tog, K1.

Work WS row.

Next Row (RS): Bind off 7 sts, work to last 3 sts, K2 tog, K1,

Work WS row.

Bind of remaining 8{7-8-7} sts.

LEFT SLEEVE

Work same as for Right Sleeve, except reverse shaping at Top of Cap by beginning shaping 1 row later, on WS row.

FINISHING

Sew Fronts to Back to Sleeves along raglan lines *(Fig. 16, page 127)*.
Sew Sleeve and side seams.

Neck Finishing: With circular needle and RS facing, beginning at Right Front edge, pick up 156{156-165-165} sts evenly along entire Neck edge *(Figs. 15a & b, page 127)*.

Cut yarn and slip all sts to opposite end of needle. Attach yarn to beginning of RS row.

Next Row (RS): Work in Shell Pattern until 8 rows are complete.

Knit 6 rows.

Bind off all sts in knit.

Left Front Band: With smaller needles and RS facing, beginning below neckline trim, pick up 94 sts to bottom.

Knit 13 rows.

Bind off all sts in knit.

Right Front Band: Work same as for Left Front Band until 4 knit rows are completed.

Instructions continued on page 48.

Next (buttonhole) Row (WS): K3, work 3-st buttonhole (by binding off 3 sts and casting on 3 sts while working bind off row), (K 16, work 3-st buttonhole) 2 times, knit to end.

Complete as for Left Front Band.

Sew buttons opposite buttonholes.

HALTER
FRONT
Cast on 83{95-105-117} sts.

Establish Patterns (RS):
Work Row 1 of Garter Stripe Pattern over 31{37-42-48} sts, place marker (PM), work Row 1 of Shell Pattern over 21 sts, PM, work Row 1 of Garter Stripe Pattern over 31{37-42-48} sts.

Work even in patterns as established until piece measures 10" (25.5 cm), end WS.

Raglan Armhole Shaping (RS): Keeping in patterns as established, bind off 5{5-6-6} sts at the beginning of the next 2 rows, then 0{2-2-2} sts at the beginning of the next 2 rows *(see Zeros, page 121)*.

Next (decrease) Row (RS):
K1, SSK, work as established to last 3 sts, K2 tog, K1.

Work WS as established.

Rep decrease row every 4th row 2{0-0-0} times, then every RS row 13{18-20-22} times more — 41{43-47-55} sts.

Next (decrease) Row (RS):
K1, SSK, knit to center panel and knit 21 sts AND AT THE SAME TIME decrease 4 sts in this section (17 sts remain), knit to last 3 sts, K2 tog, K1 — 35{37-41-49} sts.

Casing for Drawstring:
Change to smaller needles and Rev St st and work for 1" (2.5 cm) more.

Bind off all sts.

BACK
Work same as Front to Armhole.

Raglan Armhole Shaping (RS): Keeping in patterns as established, bind off 5{5-6-6} sts at the beginning of the next 2 rows, then 0{2-2-2} sts at the beginning of the next 2 rows.

Next (decrease) Row (RS):
K1, SSK, work as established to last 3 sts, K2 tog, K1.

Work WS as established.

Rep decrease row ever 4th row 2{0-0-0} times, then every RS row 16{21-23-25} times more — 35{37-41-49} sts.

Next (decrease) Row (RS):
K1, SSK, knit to center panel and knit 21 sts AND AT THE SAME TIME decrease 4 sts in this section (17 sts remain), knit to last 3 sts, K2 tog, K1 — 29{31-35-43} sts.

Casing for Drawstring:
Change to smaller needles and Rev St st and work for 1" (2.5 cm) more.

Bind off all sts.

FINISHING
Sew Front to Back at sides. Fold casings in half to WS and sew in place.

Armhole Trim: With smaller needles and RS facing, pick up 32{37-42-47} sts along Back Armhole edge, then 29{34-39-44} sts along Front Armhole edge, excluding casings — 61{71-81-91} sts.

With larger needle, bind off loosely on next row.

Rep for second armhole.

Cord: With smaller needle, cast on 150{170-190-210} sts.

Purl 1 row.

With larger needle, bind off in knit.

Attach large safety pin to end of cord and thread cord through casings. Tie at side. Sew buttons to ends of cord if desired✳

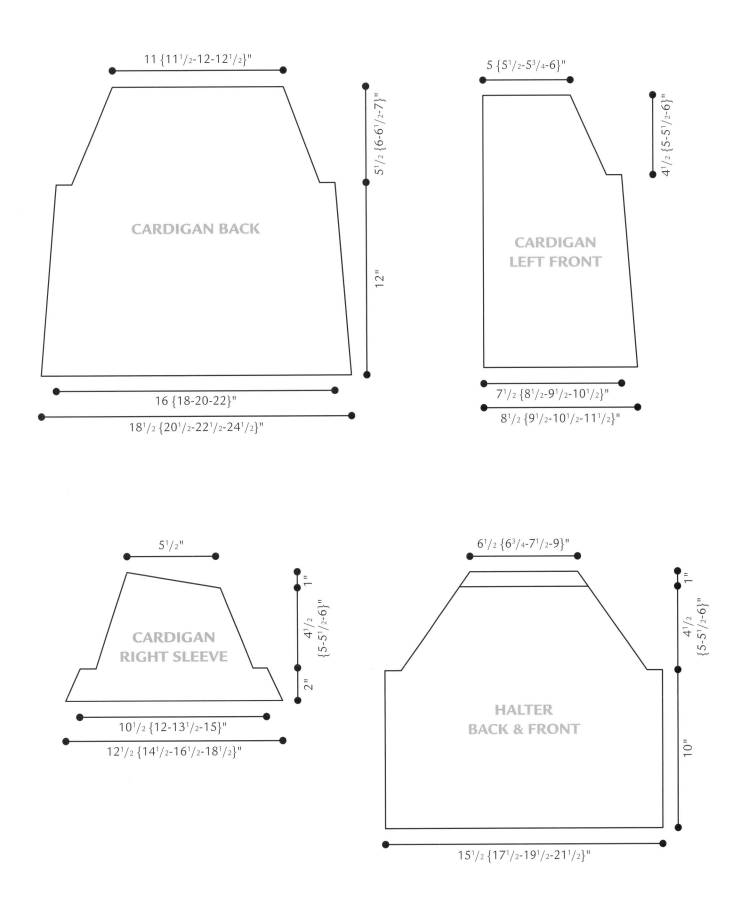

11 {11¹/₂-12-12¹/₂}"

5¹/₂ {6-6¹/₂-7}"

12"

CARDIGAN BACK

16 {18-20-22}"

18¹/₂ {20¹/₂-22¹/₂-24¹/₂}"

5 {5¹/₂-5³/₄-6}"

4¹/₂ {5-5¹/₂-6}"

CARDIGAN LEFT FRONT

7¹/₂ {8¹/₂-9¹/₂-10¹/₂}"

8¹/₂ {9¹/₂-10¹/₂-11¹/₂}"

5¹/₂"

1"

4¹/₂ {5-5¹/₂-6}"

2"

CARDIGAN RIGHT SLEEVE

10¹/₂ {12-13¹/₂-15}"

12¹/₂ {14¹/₂-16¹/₂-18¹/₂}"

6¹/₂ {6³/₄-7¹/₂-9}"

1"

4¹/₂ {5-5¹/₂-6}"

10"

HALTER BACK & FRONT

15¹/₂ {17¹/₂-19¹/₂-21¹/₂}"

Oyster's Pearl Lace
PULLOVER

▰▰▰▱ **INTERMEDIATE**

SIZES

To fit sizes Small {Medium-Large-Extra Large}
Sample in size Medium.

MEASUREMENTS

Finished bust at underarm: 32{36-40-44}"/81.5{91.5-101.5-112} cm
Length to shoulder: 22{22^1/$_2$-23-23^1/$_2$}"/56{57-58.5-59.5} cm
Sleeve width at upper arm: 11{12-13^1/$_2$-15}"/28{30.5-34.5-38} cm

Size Note: Instructions are written for size Small with sizes Medium, Large and X-Large in braces { }. Instructions will be easier to read if you circle all the numbers pertaining to your size. If only one number is given, it applies to all sizes.

✳   ✳   ✳   ✳   ✳   ✳   ✳   ✳   ✳   ✳   ✳   ✳   ✳   ✳   ✳   ✳   ✳

In BONSAI yarn from Berroco

This lace is another example, like the Lace in the VARSAILLE VACATION SHRUG on page 84, that has a very interesting texture due to the yarn-overs happening on both right side and wrong side of the knitting. I thought the scallops looked like oyster shells — oysters are a favorite treat of mine — and so I chose a bamboo-blend tape that was opalescent and pearly.

In order to use the wavelike quality to its best advantage, I decided to work the border at the lower edge from side to side. Then the front and back are picked up along the upper edge of the border. If you wanted a narrower border at the lower edge for a shorter sweater, you could work one or two repeats widthwise, instead of the three repeats in the garment.

I had a plan to button the border at the side, but when I saw how the sweater draped, I decided it was more interesting to leave the opening at the side. I found a great mother-of-pearl button with large eyes, big enough to sew the tape yarn through and add detail that way, as well.

How different this sweater would look worked in smooth, matte finished yarn! A springy cotton blend would make a firmer and less drapey fabric!

MATERIALS

BERROCO®
"Bonsai™"  **MEDIUM 4**
(97% Bamboo, 3% Nylon;
50 grams/77 yards)
   Color #4206 (Matcha):
      10{11-12-14} hanks
Straight knitting needles,
   sizes 6 (4 mm) **and**
   7 (4.5 mm) **or** sizes
   needed to obtain gauge
24" (61 cm) Circular
   knitting needle, size 6
   (4 mm)
Stitch markers
1¹⁄₈" (29 mm) Button
   with large eyes

GAUGE

Over St st using larger
needles:
20 sts and 26 rows =
4" (10 cm)
Take time to save time,
check your gauge.

Techniques used:

- YO *(Figs. 2a-d, page 122)*
- M1 *(Figs. 3a & b,*
  page 123)
- K2 tog *(Fig. 4, page 123)*
- P2 tog *(Fig. 5, page 123)*
- SSK *(Figs. 7a-c, page 124)*
- Slip 1 as if to **knit**, K2 tog,
  PSSO *(Figs. 9a & b,*
  page 125)

Instructions begin on page 52.

PATTERN STITCHES
BONSAI LACE PATTERN:
Multiple of 15 sts plus 1

Row 1 (RS): * K2, YO, SSK, YO, K2, YO, slip 1, K2 tog, PSSO, K5, P1; rep from * across to last st, K1.

Row 2: P1, * K1, P7, YO, P2 tog, K1, P2, YO, P2 tog; rep from * across.

Row 3: * K2, YO, SSK, YO, P1, K2, YO, slip 1, K2 tog, PSSO, K4, P1; rep from * across to last st, K1.

Row 4: P1, * K1, P6, YO, P2 tog, K1, P3, YO, P2 tog; rep from * across.

Row 5: * K2, YO, SSK, YO, K1, P1, K2, YO, slip 1, K2 tog, PSSO, K3, P1; rep from * across to last st, K1.

Row 6: P1, * K1, P5, YO, P2 tog, K1, P4, YO, P2 tog; rep from * across.

Row 7: * K2, YO, SSK, YO, K2 tog, YO, P1, K2, YO, slip 1, K2 tog, PSSO, K2, P1; rep from * across to last st, K1.

Row 8: P1, * K1, P4, YO, P2 tog, (K1, P2) 2 times, YO, P2 tog; rep from * across.

Row 9: * K2, YO, SSK, YO, P1, YO, SSK, P1, K2, YO, slip 1, K2 tog, PSSO, K1, P1; rep from * across to last st, K1.

Row 10: P1, * K1, P3, YO, P2 tog, K1, P2, K1, P3, YO, P2 tog; rep from * across.

Row 11: * K2, YO, SSK, YO, K1, P1, K2 tog, YO, P1, K2, YO, slip 1, K2 tog, PSSO, P1; rep from * across to last st, K1.

Row 12: P1, * K1, P2, YO, P2 tog, K1, P2, K1, P4, YO, P2 tog; rep from * across.

Row 13: * K2, YO, SSK, YO, K2 tog, YO, P1, YO, SSK, P1, K2, YO, slip 1, K2 tog, PSSO; rep from * across to last st, K1.

Row 14: P1, * P2, YO, P2 tog, (K1, P2) 3 times, YO, P2 tog; repeat from * across.

Row 15: * K2, (YO, SSK, P1) 2 times, K2 tog, YO, K2 tog, K1, YO, SSK, YO; rep from * across to last st, K1.

Row 16: P1, * P3, YO, P2 tog, P2, (K1, P2) 2 times, YO, P2 tog; rep from * across.

Row 17: * K2, YO, SSK, P1, K2 tog, YO, P1, YO, slip 1, K2 tog, PSSO, K1, YO, SSK, YO, K1; rep from * across to last st, K1.

Row 18: P1, * P4, YO, P2 tog, P1, (K1, P2) 2 times, YO, P2 tog; rep from * across.

Row 19: * K2, YO, SSK, P1, YO, SSK, P1, K2 tog, K1, YO, SSK, YO, K2; rep from * across to last st, K1.

Row 20: P1, * P5, YO, P2 tog, (K1, P2) 2 times, YO, P2 tog; rep from * across.

Row 21: * K2, YO, SSK, P1, K2 tog, YO, K2 tog, K1, YO, SSK, YO, K3; rep from * across to last st, K1.

Row 22: P1, * P6, YO, P2 tog, P2, K1, P2, YO, P2 tog; rep from * across.

Row 23: * K2, YO, SSK, P1, YO, slip 1, K2 tog, PSSO, K1, YO, SSK, YO, K4; rep from * across to last st, K1.

Row 24: P1, * P7, YO, P2 tog, P1, K1, P2, YO, P2 tog; rep from * across.

Row 25: * K2, YO, SSK, P1, K2 tog, K1, YO, SSK, YO, K5; rep from * across to last st, K1.

Row 26: P1, * P8, YO, P2 tog, K1, P2, YO, P2 tog; rep from * across.

Row 27: * K2, YO, SSK, K2 tog, K1, YO, SSK, YO, K6; rep from * across to last st, K1.

Row 28: P1, * P9, YO, P2 tog, P2, YO, P2 tog; rep from * across.

Rep Rows 1-28 for Bonsai Lace Pattern.

EYELET GARTER RIB:
Multiple of 4 sts plus 3

Rows 1, 3, 5 and 7 (RS): K3, * P1, K3; rep from * across.

Rows 2, 4, 6 and 8 (WS): Purl across.

Row 9: K3, * YO, SSK, K2; rep from * across.

Row 10: Purl across.

Rep Rows 1-10 for Eyelet Garter Rib.

STOCKINETTE STITCH
(St st): Any number of sts

Knit RS rows, purl WS rows.

LOWER BODY BORDER

With larger needles, cast on 48 sts.

Establish Pattern (RS):
K1 (edge st), work Row 1 of Bonsai Lace Pattern over 46 sts, K1 (edge st).

Keeping edge st each side in St st, work as established until piece measures 7{8-9-10}"/ 18{20.5-23-25.5} cm.

Tie a marker at the beginning and the end of last row.

Continue as established until piece measures 14{16-18-20}"/ 35.5{40.5-45.5-51} cm, end WS.

Bind off all sts in knit.

FRONT

With RS facing and larger needles, pick up 71{81-91-101} sts evenly along straight edge of Lower Body Border from cast on edge to center marker *(Figs. 15a & b, page 127)*.

Purl WS row.

Establish Patterns (RS):
Work 5{10-15-20} sts in St st, place marker (PM) *(see Markers, page 121)*, work Row 1 of Eyelet Garter Rib over 15 sts, PM, work Row 1 of Bonsai Lace Pattern over 31 sts, PM, work Row 1 of Eyelet Garter Rib over 15 sts, PM, work remaining 5{10-15-20} sts in St st.

Instructions continued on page 54.

Work as established for 5 rows more.

Next (increase) Row (RS):
K2, M1, work as established across to last 2 sts, M1, K2 — 73{83-93-103} sts.

Working increases into St st, rep increase row every 6th row 4 times more — 81{91-101-111} sts.

Work even until piece measures 15" (38 cm) from beginning, end WS.

Armhole Shaping (RS):
Bind off 5 sts at the beginning of next the 2 rows, then 0{0-2-2} sts at the beginning of next the 2 rows *(see Zeros, page 121)* — 71{81-87-97} sts.

Next (decrease) Row (RS):
K1, SSK, work in patterns across to last 3 sts, K2 tog, K1 — 69{79-85-95} sts.

WS Rows: P1, work to last st, P1.

Rep decrease row every RS row 3{5-6-8} times — 63{69-73-79} sts.

Work even until Armholes measure 4$^{1}/_{2}${5-5$^{1}/_{2}$-6}"/ 11.5{12.5-14-15} cm, end WS.

Front Neck Shaping (RS):
Mark center 27{27-31-31} sts. Work to marker; join a second ball of yarn and bind off center marked sts, work to end — 18{21-21-24} sts each side.

Working both sides at once, bind off at each Neck edge, 3 sts once, then 2 sts 3 times — 9{12-12-15} sts each side.

Work even until Armholes measure 7{7$^{1}/_{2}$-8-8$^{1}/_{2}$}"/ 18{19-20.5-21.5} cm, end WS.

Shoulder Shaping (RS):
Bind off 3{4-4-5} sts at the beginning of the next 6 rows.

BACK

With larger needles, pick up 71{81-91-101} sts evenly along straight edge of Lower Body Border, beginning in same st as last st of Front to bound off edge.

Purl WS row.

Work as for Front until Armholes measure 5$^{1}/_{2}${6-6$^{1}/_{2}$-7}"/ 14{15-16.5-18} cm, end WS — 63{69-73-79} sts.

Back Neck Shaping (RS):
Mark center 31{31-35-35} sts. Work to marker; join a second ball of yarn and bind off center marked sts, work to end — 16{19-19-22} sts each side.

Working both sides at once, bind off at each Neck edge, 3 sts once, then 2 sts twice — 9{12-12-15} sts each side.

When piece measures same as Front to shoulder, work Shoulder Shaping as for Front.

SLEEVES
LOWER SLEEVE BORDER

With larger needles, cast on 18 sts.

Establish Pattern (RS):
K1 (edge st), work Row 1 of Bonsai Lace Pattern over 16 sts, K1 (edge st).

Keeping edge st each side in St st, work as established until piece measures 11{12-13$^{1}/_{2}$-15}"/ 28{30.5-34.5-38} cm, end WS.

Bind off all sts in knit.

UPPER SLEEVE

With RS facing and larger needles, pick up 57{61-69-77} sts evenly along straight edge of Lower Sleeve Border.

Purl WS row.

Establish Pattern (RS):
K1 (edge st), work Row 1 of Eyelet Garter Rib to last st, K1 (edge st).

Keeping edge st each side in St st, work as established until piece measures 8" (20.5 cm) from beginning, end WS.

Armhole Shaping (RS):
Bind off 5 sts at the beginning of the next 2 rows, then 0{0-2-2} sts at the beginning of the next 2 rows — 47{51-55-63} sts.

Next (decrease) Row (RS):
K1, SSK, work in pattern to last 3 sts, K2 tog, K1 — 45{49-53-61} sts.

WS Rows: P1, work to last st, P1.

Rep decrease row every RS row 13{15-15-16} times — 19{19-23-29} sts.

Bind off 2 sts at the beginning of the next 2{2-4-4} rows, then 0{0-0-3} sts at the beginning of the next 2 rows — 15 sts.

Bind off remaining sts.

FINISHING

Sew Back to Front at shoulders.
Sew in Sleeves. Sew Sleeve seams.
Sew side seams under arms, leaving open left Lower Body Border side unsewn.

Neck Finishing: With circular needle and RS facing, beginning at right shoulder, pick up 44{44-48-48} sts evenly along Back Neck edge, then 52{52-56-56} sts evenly along Front Neck edge; place marker and join — 96{96-104-104} sts.

P1 rnd, K1 rnd, P1 rnd.

Bind off all sts in knit.

Front Lace Border Trim: With smaller needles, pick up 44 sts evenly along Front cast-on edge of Lower Body Border.

Knit 3 rows.

Bind off all sts in knit.

Back Lace Border Trim: Measure 1" (2.5 cm) down from body section of back bound-off edge of Lower Body Border. With smaller needle, pick up 40 sts along edge.

Knit 3 rows.

Bind off all sts in knit.

Overlap Front trim over back at top and sew untrimmed edge underneath.
Sew button through all layers. ✳

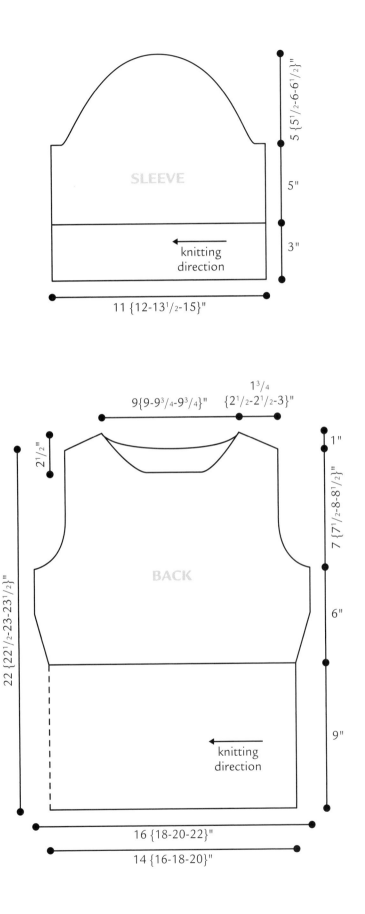

SLEEVE

knitting direction

5 {5¹/₂-6-6¹/₂}"

5"

3"

11 {12-13¹/₂-15}"

BACK

knitting direction

9{9-9³/₄-9³/₄}"

1³/₄ {2¹/₂-2¹/₂-3}"

2¹/₂"

1"

7 {7¹/₂-8-8¹/₂}"

6"

9"

22 {22¹/₂-23-23¹/₂}"

16 {18-20-22}"

14 {16-18-20}"

Peridot DRESS

⬛⬛⬛◻ **INTERMEDIATE**

SIZES
To fit sizes Extra Small {Small-Medium-Large}
Sample in size Small.

MEASUREMENTS
Finished bust at underarm: 32{36-40-44}"/81.5{91.5-101.5-112} cm
Length to shoulder: 35^1/$_2${36-36^1/$_2$-37}"/90{91.5-92.5-94} cm

Size Note: Instructions are written for size X-Small with sizes Small, Medium and Large in braces { }. Instructions will be easier to read if you circle all the numbers pertaining to your size. If only one number is given, it applies to all sizes.

✳ ✳ ✳ ✳ ✳ ✳ ✳ ✳ ✳ ✳ ✳ ✳ ✳ ✳ ✳ ✳ ✳

In SPA from Caron International
This design, worked in a smooth silky synthetic and bamboo blend has the pretty sheen of a gemstone! And it has the drape and refinement of a dressy-dress as well as the wear-ability of an everyday garment. It would work as a jumper too, with a featherweight tee underneath. The border at the lower edge accentuates the bell-shape.

This dress could be shortened to tunic length by simply working fewer rows between the decreases that narrow the pieces.

You could also work this in any number of lightweight summer yarns. Avoid heavier yarns/fibers that might cause the dress to sag, unless you plan to shorten it. If you would like to add sleeves — use the sleeve pattern from the white linen tunic on page 82.

Instructions begin on page 58.

MATERIALS

CARON **(LIGHT 3)** INTERNATIONAL "Spa"
(75% Microdenier Acrylic, 25% Bamboo;
85 grams/251 yards)
   Color #04 (Green Sheen):
      4{5-5-6} skeins
Straight knitting needles,
   size 7 (4.5 mm) **or** size
   needed to obtain gauge
24" (61 cm) Circular
   knitting needle, size 6
   (4 mm) for finishing
Stitch markers
2 Distinctive markers

GAUGE

Over St st: 22 sts and
28 rows = 4" (10 cm)
Over Garter Ridge Pattern:
24 sts and 22 rows =
4" (10 cm)
Lace Panel over 17 sts =
3" (7.5 cm) wide
Take time to save time,
check your gauge.

Techniques used:

- YO (**Fig. 2a, page 122**)
- K2 tog (**Fig. 4, page 123**)
- SSK (**Figs. 7a-c, page 124**)
- Slip 1 as if to **knit**, K2 tog,
  PSSO (**Figs. 9a & b,
  page 125**)

PATTERN STITCHES
STOCKINETTE STITCH
(St st): Any number of sts

Knit RS rows, purl WS rows.

GARTER STITCH: Any number of sts

Knit every row.

GARTER RIDGE PATTERN: Multiple of 10 sts

Right Twist (RT): K2 tog but do not slip st from needle; insert RH needle between the sts just knitted together, and knit the first st again; then drop both sts from LH needle tog.

Left Twist (LT): Insert RH needle in back of 2nd st on LH needle, then knit this st, do not drop sts, then knit first st as usual; then drop both sts from LH needle tog.

Row 1 (RS): Knit across.
Row 2 (WS): * K4, P2, K4; rep from * across.
Row 3: * K3, RT, LT, K3; rep from * across.
Row 4: Purl across.
Rep Rows 1-4 for Garter Ridge Pattern.

LACE PANEL: Panel of 17 sts

Row 1 (RS): K1, YO, K3, SSK, P5, K2 tog, K3, YO, K1.
Row 2: P6, K5, P6.
Row 3: K2, YO, K3, SSK, P3, K2 tog, K3, YO, K2.
Row 4: P7, K3, P7.
Row 5: K3, YO, K3, SSK, P1, K2 tog, K3, YO, K3.
Row 6: P8, K1, P8.
Row 7: K4, YO, K3, slip 1, K2 tog, PSSO, K3, YO, K4.
Row 8: Purl across.
Rep Rows 1-8 for Lace Panel.

BACK

Cast on 122{132-142-152} sts.

Establish Pattern (RS):
K1 (edge st), work in Garter Ridge Pattern over 120{130-140-150} sts, K1 (edge st).

Keeping edge sts in St st, work as established for approximately 4" (10 cm), ending with Row 3 of pattern.

Purl WS row decreasing 13{13-11-11} sts evenly spaced across (**see Increasing and Decreasing Evenly Across A Row, page 123**) — 109{119-131-141} sts.

Establish Patterns (RS):
Work 19{24-30-35} sts in St st, place marker (PM) (**see Markers, page 121**), work 2 sts in Garter st, PM, work Row 1 of Lace Panel over 17 sts, place first distinctive marker, work 6 sts in St st, PM, work 2 sts in Garter st, PM, work Row 1 of Lace Panel over center 17 sts, PM, work 2 sts in Garter st, PM, work 6 sts in St st, place second distinctive marker, work Row 1 of Lace Panel over 17 sts, PM, work 2 sts in Garter st, PM, work remaining 19{24-30-35} sts in St st.

Work even in patterns as established until 24 rows are complete, ending WS.

Instructions continued on page 60.

Next (decrease) Row (RS):
K3, SSK, work to first distinctive marker, slip marker, SSK, work as established to 2 sts before second distinctive marker, K2 tog, slip marker and work as established to last 5 sts, K2 tog, K3.

Rep decrease row every 24th row 4 times more — 89{99-111-121} sts.

Work even until piece measures 29" (73.5 cm), end WS.

Armhole Shaping (RS):
Bind off 3{3-4-4} sts at the beginning of the next 2 rows, then 2 sts at the beginning of the next 8{12-14-16} rows — 67{69-75-81} sts.

Work even in patterns until Armholes measure 4{4^1/$_2$-5-5^1/$_2$}"/ 10{11.5-12.5-14} cm, end WS.

Back Neck Shaping (RS):
Mark center 17{17-21-23} sts. Work to marker; join a second ball of yarn and bind off center marked sts, work to end — 25{26-27-29} sts each side.

Working both sides at once, bind off from each Neck edge 3 sts 6 times — 7{8-9-11} sts each side.

Work even until Armholes measure 6^1/$_2${7-7^1/$_2$-8}"/ 16.5{18-19-20.5} cm, end WS.

Bind off 7{8-9-11} sts from each shoulder.

FRONT

Work as for Back until Armholes measure 2$\frac{1}{2}${3-3$\frac{1}{2}$-4}"/ 6.5{7.5-9-10} cm, end WS.

Work same Neck Shaping as for Back — 7{8-9-11} sts each side.

Work even until Armholes measure 6$\frac{1}{2}${7-7$\frac{1}{2}$-8}"/ 16.5{18-19-20.5} cm, end WS.

Bind off 7{8-9-11} sts from each shoulder.

FINISHING

Sew Front to Back at shoulders.

Armhole Trim: With circular needle and RS facing, pick up 82{86-92-96} sts evenly along Armhole edge (*Figs. 15a & b, page 127*).

Working back and forth, knit 5 rows.

Bind off all sts in knit.

Neckline Trim: With circular needle and RS facing, starting at back right shoulder seam, pick up 57{57-60-63} sts along Back Neck edge to shoulder, then 74{74-78-82} sts along Front Neck edge to beginning; place marker and join.

(K1 rnd, P1 rnd) 3 times.

Bind off all sts in knit.

Sew side seams including Armhole Trim (*Fig. 16, page 127*).

Lower Edge Trim: With circular needle and RS facing, starting at side seam, pick up 1 st for every cast on st along entire lower edge, not including seam sts; place marker and join.

P1 rnd, K1 rnd, P1 rnd.

Bind off all sts in knit. ✳

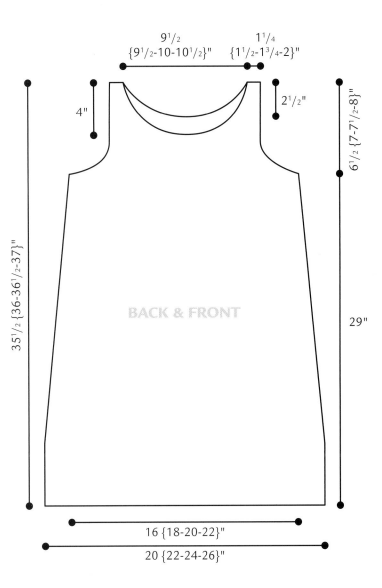

9$\frac{1}{2}$ {9$\frac{1}{2}$-10-10$\frac{1}{2}$}"

1$\frac{1}{4}$ {1$\frac{1}{2}$-1$\frac{3}{4}$-2}"

4"

2$\frac{1}{2}$"

6$\frac{1}{2}$ {7-7$\frac{1}{2}$-8}"

35$\frac{1}{2}$ {36-36$\frac{1}{2}$-37}"

BACK & FRONT

29"

16 {18-20-22}"

20 {22-24-26}"

Sand Shadows
TWIN SET

 **INTERMEDIATE**

SIZES

To fit sizes Small {Medium-Large-Extra Large}
Sample in size Small.

MEASUREMENTS

Tank top:
Finished bust at underarm: 36{40-44-48}"/91.5{101.5-112-122} cm
Length to shoulder: 21{21^1/$_2$-22-22^1/$_2$}"/53.5{54.5-56-57} cm
Cardigan:
Finished bust at underarm: 38{42-46-50}"/96.5{106.5-117-127} cm
Length to shoulder: 25{25^1/$_2$-26-26^1/$_2$}"/63.5{65-66-67.5} cm
Sleeve width at upper arm: 12{13-14^1/$_2$-16}"/30.5{33-37-40.5} cm

Size Note: Instructions are written for size Small with sizes Medium, Large
and X-Large in braces { }. Instructions will be easier to read if you circle all the
numbers pertaining to your size. If only one number is given, it applies to all sizes.

❊　❊　❊　❊　❊　❊　❊　❊　❊　❊　❊　❊　❊　❊　❊　❊　❊　❊　❊

In SAHARA yarn from Stacy Charles
Tank Top & Cardigan
Although this set has a heavy drape to it, the fabric is anything but warm! Three of summer's coolest
fibers — viscose, bamboo and linen — come together in a sheer ribbon "yarn" that is cool and knits to
a deeply textured fabric that slides on the skin and swings away from the body. I chose patterns that
accentuated the natural color, lent a tone-on-tone feel, and the quality of shifting sand. A simple 4-row
slipped-stitch cable has a loop-like structure to show off the ribbon-y quality of the yarn. I planned the
simplest reverse stockinette stitch and my favorite pattern of all time, simple seed stitch, as textured
background.

This twin set features a tank that is the same piece front and back. And the cardigan is long and drapey
in contrast. Both pieces are comfortable, worn alone or together. You might vary the look by making the
tank longer and the cardigan shorter; or add a shortened version of the cardigan sleeve to the tank! Or
eliminate the sleeve on the cardigan to create a long vest!

I searched high and low for perfect buttons — a mania of mine — and found these 60's inspired bamboo
cut-outs that look like a single flower from the huge clusters of my mother's "Annabel" hydrangea.

Instructions begin on page 64.

MATERIALS

STACY CHARLES "Sahara" [MEDIUM 4]
(44% Viscose,
36% Bamboo, 20% Linen;
50 grams/87 yards)
Color #02 (Sand)
  Tank: 7{7-8-9} balls
  Cardigan:
    12{14-15-17} balls
Straight knitting needles,
  sizes 7 (4.5 mm) **and**
  9 (5.5 mm) **or** sizes
  needed to obtain gauge
24" (61 cm) Circular
  needle, size 7 (4.5 mm)
Cable needle (cn)
Markers
1" (25 mm) Buttons - 4
Yarn needle

GAUGE

Over Rev St st with larger
needles: 18 sts and
29 rows = 4" (10 cm)
Take time to save time,
check your gauge.

Techniques used:

- K2 tog *(Fig. 4, page 123)*
- P2 tog *(Fig. 5, page 123)*
- SSK *(Figs. 7a-c, page 124)*
- M1 *(Figs. 3a & b, page 123)*

PATTERN STITCHES

REVERSE STOCKINETTE STITCH (Rev St st): Any number of sts
Purl RS rows, knit WS rows.

STOCKINETTE STITCH (St st): Any number of sts
Knit RS rows, purl WS rows.

SEED STITCH: Odd number of sts
All rows: P1, * K1, P1; rep from * across.

SLIPPED STITCH CABLE: (Panel of 9 sts)
Preparatory Row (RS): P2, K2 winding the yarn twice around needle for each st, P1, K2 winding the yarn twice around needle for each st, P2.

Row 1 (WS): K2, bring yarn to the front, slip 2 with yarn in front (wyif) letting loops drop, bring yarn to the back, K1, bring yarn to the front, slip 2 wyif letting loops drop, bring yarn to the back, K2.
Rows 2 and 3: Knit the knit sts and purl the purl sts as they present themselves, and slip the slipped sts of previous row with yarn at the WS of fabric.
Row 4 (Cable cross row): Slip 2 sts to cn and hold in back, K2, then K2 from cn winding the yarn twice around needle for each st, P1, slip 2 sts to cn and hold in front, K2 winding the yarn twice around needle for each st, then K2 from cn.
Rep Rows 1-4 for Slipped St Cable.

TANK TOP
BACK AND FRONT

With larger needles, cast on 93{101-109-117} sts.

Preparatory Row (RS):
K2 (edge sts), place marker (PM) *(see Markers, page 121)*, K 13{17-21-25}, PM, work Preparatory Row of Cable over 9 sts, PM, (K9, PM, work Preparatory Row of Cable over 9 sts, PM) 3 times, K 13{17-21-25}, PM, K2 (edge sts).

* Establish Patterns (WS):
P2 (edge sts), slip marker, work 13{17-21-25} sts in Rev St st, slip marker, work Row 1 of Cable over 9 sts, slip marker, (work 9 sts in Rev St st, slip marker, work Row 1 of Cable over 9 sts, slip marker) 3 times, work 13{17-21-25} sts in Rev St st, P2 (edge sts).

Keeping 2 edge sts in St st, work even as established until Rows 1-4 of Cable have been worked 4 times.

Change Patterns (WS):
P2, slip marker, work 13{17-21-25} sts in Seed st, work Row 1 of Cable over 9 sts, (work 9 sts in Seed st, work Row 1 of Cable over 9 sts) 3 times, work 13{17-21-25} sts in Seed st, P2.

Work even as established until Rows 1-4 of Cable have been worked 4 times.

Rep from * for remainder of piece AND AT THE SAME TIME, work until piece measures 14" (35.5 cm), end WS.

Armhole Shaping (RS):
Keeping in patterns as established, bind off 4 sts at the beginning of the next 2 rows, then 0{0-2-2} sts at the beginning of the next 2 rows *(see Zeros, page 121)*.

Next (decrease) Row (RS):
SSK, work to last 2 sts, K2 tog.

WS Rows: P1, work as established to last st, P1.

Rep decrease row every RS row 3{5-4-9} times more, then every 4th row 5{5-5-2} times AND AT THE SAME TIME, when Armholes measure approximately 2{2^1/$_2$-3-3^1/$_2$}"/ 5{6.5-7.5-9} cm, end with Row 3 of Cable Pattern.

Neck Shaping (RS):
Mark center 23 sts. Work as established to center 23 sts; join a second ball of yarn and bind off center 23 sts (omitting the double wraps in Cable Pattern), work to end.

Working both sides at the same time and keeping in pattern, work WS row.

Neck (decrease) Row (RS):
Continue Armhole decreases if necessary AND AT THE SAME TIME, at each Neck edge, bind off 2 sts once, then decrease 1 st every RS row 4 times, then every 4th row 4 times — 12{14-17-19} sts remaining each side.

Instructions continued on page 66.

Work even until Armholes measure approximately 7{7$\frac{1}{2}$-8-8$\frac{1}{2}$}"/ 18{19-20.5-21.5} cm, ending with Row 3 of Cable Pattern.

Shoulder Shaping (RS): Bind off 12{14-17-19} sts each side (omitting the double wraps in Cable Pattern).

FINISHING
Sew Back to Front at shoulders.

Armhole Trim: With smaller needles and RS facing, pick up 72{76-80-84} sts evenly along entire Armhole edge *(Figs. 15a & b, page 127)*.

Knit WS row.

Bind off all sts in knit.

Repeat for second Armhole.

Sew side seams *(Fig. 16, page 127)*.

Neckline Trim: With circular needle and RS facing, pick up 112 sts evenly around neckline; place marker and join.

Purl 1 rnd.

Bind off all sts in knit.

Lower Edge Trim: With circular needle and RS facing, pick up 1 st for every cast-on st, excluding seam sts along lower edge; place marker and join.

Purl 1 rnd.

Bind off all sts in knit.

Steam lower edge lightly to enhance scalloped effect.

CARDIGAN
BACK
With larger needles, cast on 97{105-117-125} sts.

Preparatory Row (RS): K2 (edge sts), PM, K 27{31-37-41} sts, PM, work Preparatory Row of Cable over 9 sts, PM, K 21 center sts, PM, work Preparatory Row of Cable over 9 sts, PM, K 27{31-37-41} sts, PM, K2 (edge sts).

* Established Patterns (WS): P2 (edge sts), work 27{31-37-41} sts in Rev St st, work Row 1 of Cable over 9 sts, work 21 sts in Rev St st, work Row 1 of Cable over 9 sts, work 27{31-37-41} sts in Rev St st, P2 (edge sts).

Keeping 2 edge sts in St st, work even as established until Rows 1-4 of Cable have been worked 4 times.

Change Patterns (WS): P2, work 27{31-37-41} sts in Seed st, work Row 1 of Cable over 9 sts, work 21 sts in Seed st, work Row 1 of Cable over 9 sts, work 27{31-37-41} sts in Seed st, P2.

Work even as established until Rows 1-4 of Cable have been worked 4 times.

Rep from * for remainder of piece AND AT THE SAME TIME, work until piece measures 17$\frac{1}{2}$" (44.5 cm), end WS.

Armhole Shaping (RS): Keeping in patterns as established, bind off 4 sts at the beginning of the next 2 rows.

Next (decrease) Row (RS): SSK, work to last 2 sts, K2 tog.

WS Rows: P1, work as established to last st, P1.

Rep decrease row every RS row 7{8-11-12} times more — 73{79-85-91} sts.

Work even until Armholes measure approximately 7$\frac{1}{2}${8-8$\frac{1}{2}$-9}"/ 19{20.5-21.5-23} cm, end with Row 3 of Cable Pattern.

Back Neck Shaping (RS): Mark center 37{39-41-43} sts. Work as established to center marker; join a second ball of yarn and bind off center 37{39-41-43} sts (omitting the double wraps in Cable Pattern), work to end — 18{20-22-24} sts each side.

Shoulder Shaping: From each shoulder edge, bind off 6{7-7-8} sts 3{2-2-3} times, then 0{6-8-0} sts 0{1-1-0} time(s).

LEFT FRONT

With larger needles,
cast on 50{54-60-64} sts.

Preparatory Row (RS):
K2 (edge sts), PM,
K 29{33-39-43}, PM, work
Preparatory Row of Cable over
9 sts, PM, K9, PM,
K1 (front edge st).

Establish Pattern (WS):
P1 (front edge st), work 9 sts
in Rev St st, slip marker, work
Row 1 of Cable over 9 sts, work
29{33-39-43} sts in Rev St st,
P2 (edge sts).

Work same pattern changes as
for Back and work until piece
measures 15" (38 cm), end WS.

**V-Neck Shaping (decrease)
and move Cable Row (RS):**
K2, slip marker, work to 2 sts
before next marker, P2 tog, slip
marker, work Cable over 9 sts,
slip marker, M1, work to last
2 sts, K2 tog.

WS Rows: P1, work sts as
established to last 2 sts, P2.

Rep decrease and move Cable
row alternately every 4th and
2nd row 17{18-19-20} times
more AND AT THE SAME TIME,
when piece measures
17 1/2" (44.5 cm), end WS.

Instructions continued on page 68.

Instructions continued on page 68.

Armhole Shaping (RS):

Keeping in patterns as established, continue Neck Shaping and movement of cable, bind off 4 sts at the beginning of the row.

WS Rows: P1, work as established to last st, P1.

Next (decrease) Row (RS): SSK, work to end.

Rep decrease row every RS row 7{8-11-12} times more AND AT THE SAME TIME, work even until Armhole measures approximately $7\frac{1}{2}${8-8$\frac{1}{2}$-9}"/ 19{20.5-21.5-23} cm, end with Row 3 of Cable — 20{22-24-26} sts.

Note: This is different # of sts as for Back shoulder.

Shoulder Shaping: From shoulder edge, bind off 10 sts once (omitting the double wraps in Cable Pattern), then bind off 5{6-7-8} sts twice.

RIGHT FRONT

Work same as for Left Front, reversing pattern placement and all shaping.

SLEEVES

With larger needles, cast on 51{55-57-61} sts.

Preparatory Row (RS): K2 (edge sts), PM, K 10{12-13-15}, PM, work Preparatory Row of Cable over 9 sts, PM, K9, PM, work Preparatory Row of Cable over 9 sts, PM, K 10{12-13-15}, PM, K2 (edge sts).

Establish Patterns (WS): P2 (edge sts), work 10{12-13-15} sts in Rev St st, work Row 1 of Cable over 9 sts, slip marker, work 9 sts in Rev St st, work Row 1 of Cable over 9 sts, slip marker, work 10{12-13-15} sts in Rev St st, P2 (edge sts).

Keeping 2 edge sts each side in St st, work same pattern changes as for Back.

Next (increase) Row (RS): K2, M1, work to last 2 sts, M1, K2.

Working increases in pattern as established, rep increase row every 10th{10th-10th-8th} row 5{5-7-8} times more — 63{67-73-79} sts.

Work as established until piece measures approximately $11\frac{1}{2}$" (29 cm), end WS.

Cap Shaping (RS): Bind off 4 sts at the beginning of the next 2 rows.

Next (decrease) Row (RS): SSK, work to last 2 sts, K2 tog.

WS Rows: P1, work as established to last st, P1.

Rep decrease row every RS row 15{17-20-23} times more.

Bind off remaining 23 sts.

FINISHING

Sew Back to Front at shoulders.
Sew in Sleeves.
Sew side and Sleeve seams.

Neckline Trim: With smaller needles and RS facing, beginning at V-Neck shaping of Right Front, pick up 54{56-58-60} sts to shoulder, 34{36-38-40} sts along Back Neck, then 54{56-58-60} sts to beginning of V-Neck shaping on Left Front — 142{148-154-160} sts.

Knit WS row. Bind off in knit, then without cutting yarn, pick up 74 sts to lower edge.

Knit 1 row. Bind off in knit, then without cutting yarn, pick up 1 st for every cast-on st, excluding seam sts, evenly along entire lower edge.

Knit 1 row. Bind off in knit, then without cutting yarn, pick up 74 sts to beginning of V-Neck shaping on Right Front. Turn.

Buttonhole Row (WS): K3, make 3-st buttonhole (by binding off 3 sts and casting on 3 sts while working bind off row), * K 12, make 3-st buttonhole; rep from * 2 times more, knit to end.

Bind off all sts in knit.

Sew buttons opposite buttonholes.

Steam lightly. ✳

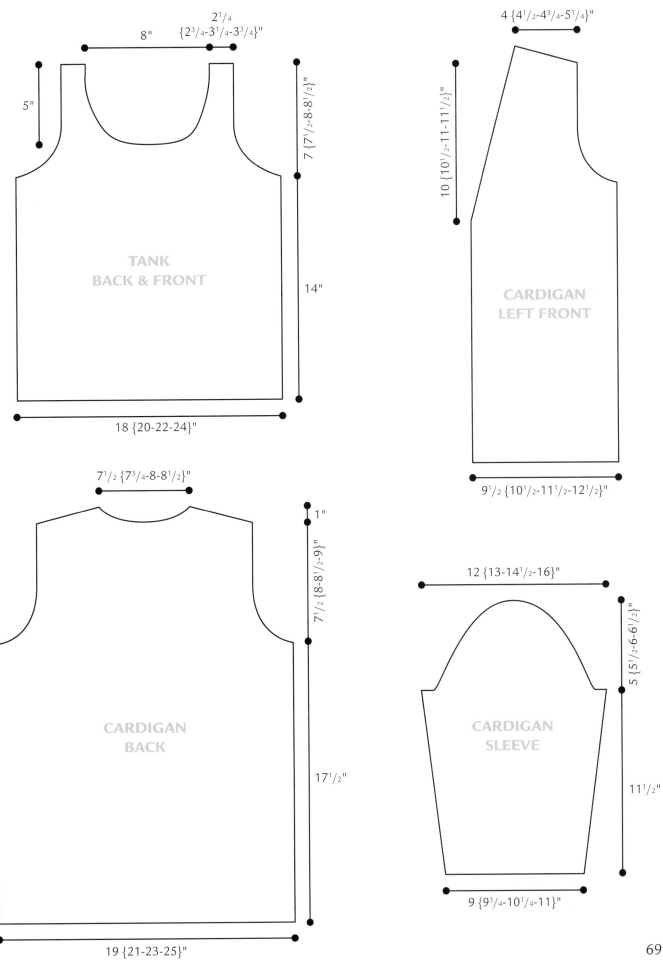

TANK
BACK & FRONT

8"

2¹/₄
{2³/₄-3¹/₄-3³/₄}"

5"

7 {7¹/₂-8-8¹/₂}"

14"

18 {20-22-24}"

CARDIGAN
LEFT FRONT

4 {4¹/₂-4³/₄-5¹/₄}"

10 {10¹/₂-11-11¹/₂}"

9¹/₂ {10¹/₂-11¹/₂-12¹/₂}"

CARDIGAN
BACK

7¹/₂ {7³/₄-8-8¹/₂}"

1"

7¹/₂ {8-8¹/₂-9}"

17¹/₂"

19 {21-23-25}"

CARDIGAN
SLEEVE

12 {13-14¹/₂-16}"

5 {5¹/₂-6-6¹/₂}"

11¹/₂"

9 {9³/₄-10¹/₄-11}"

Twilight Trellis
CARDI

◖■■■▢ INTERMEDIATE

SIZES
To fit sizes Small {Medium-Large-Extra Large}
Sample in size Medium.

MEASUREMENTS
Finished bust at underarm: 32{37-41-46}"/81.5{94-104-117} cm
Length to shoulder: 21{21¹/₂-22-22¹/₂}"/53.5{54.5-56-57} cm
Sleeve width at upper arm: 12{12-13-14}"/30.5{30.5-33-35.5} cm

Size Note: Instructions are written for size Small with sizes Medium, Large and X-Large in braces { }. Instructions will be easier to read if you circle all the numbers pertaining to your size. If only one number is given, it applies to all sizes.

✳   ✳   ✳   ✳   ✳   ✳   ✳   ✳   ✳   ✳   ✳   ✳   ✳   ✳   ✳   ✳   ✳   ✳

In CREATIVE FOCUS COTTON yarn from Nashua Handknits
I wanted this cardi to have a 40's feel, with a slightly puffed sleeve. I love the crisp lines of ribs that are made of single twisted stitches on a background of reverse stockinette stitch, and I incorporated a "wrong-side" lace pattern to work within the ribs, as a border of sorts. It has a trellis-like shape, like the one I grow summer moon-vines on in my driveway, and so my obvious choice of buttons!

This 100% hard-twisted cotton has intense color and is a cool choice for a summer garment. Not soft and clingy, it stands away from the body crisply, and it also holds the more structured shape of this cardigan. I like the gentle drawing-in of the ribs, not too close-fitting, but slightly seeking the feminine curves. If you choose a softer yarn, the sweater will cling and drape more.

Instructions begin on page 72.

MATERIALS

NASHUA HANDKNITS "Creative Focus Cotton" MEDIUM 4
(100% Mercerized Cotton; 50 grams/93 yards)
Color #014 (Dried Lavender): 9{10-11-12} skeins
Straight knitting needles, sizes 6 (4 mm) **and** 7 (4.5 mm) **or** sizes needed to obtain gauge
Stitch markers
1" (25 mm) Buttons - 3

GAUGE

Over Lace Pattern using larger needles:
21 sts and 26 rows = 4" (10 cm)
Take time to save time, check your gauge.

Techniques used:

- K1 tbl and P1 tbl **(Fig. 12, page 126)**
- YO **(Figs. 2b-d, page 122)**
- K2 tog **(Fig. 4, page 123)**
- P2 tog **(Fig. 5, page 123)**
- P2 tog tbl **(Fig. 6, page 124)**
- SSK **(Figs. 7a-c, page 124)**
- Slip 2 tog as if to **knit**, K1, P2SSO **(Figs. 10a & b, page 125)**

PATTERN STITCHES
LACE PATTERN: Multiple of 12 sts plus 1

Row 1 (RS): * K1 tbl, YO, P2 tog tbl, P3, K1 tbl, P3, P2 tog, YO; rep from * across to last st, K1 tbl.

Row 2 and all WS rows: * P1 tbl, K5; rep from * to last st, P1 tbl.

Row 3: * K1 tbl, P1, YO, P2 tog tbl, P2, K1 tbl, P2, P2 tog, YO, P1; rep from * to last st, K1 tbl.

Row 5: * K1 tbl, P2, YO, P2 tog tbl, P1, K1 tbl, P1, P2 tog, YO, P2; rep from * to last st, K1 tbl.

Row 7: * K1 tbl, P3, YO, P2 tog tbl, K1 tbl, P2 tog, YO, P3; rep from * across to last st, K1 tbl.

Row 9: * K1 tbl, P4, YO, slip 2, K1, P2SSO, YO, P4; rep from * across to last st, K1 tbl.

Row 11: * K1 tbl, P3, P2 tog, YO, K1 tbl, YO, P2 tog tbl, P3; rep from * across to last st, K1 tbl.

Row 13: * K1 tbl, P2, P2 tog, YO, P1, K1 tbl, P1, YO, P2 tog tbl, P2; rep from * across to last st, K1 tbl.

Row 15: * K1 tbl, P1, P2 tog, YO, P2, K1 tbl, P2, YO, P2 tog tbl, P1; rep from * to last st K1 tbl.

Row 17: * K1 tbl, P2 tog, YO, P3, K1 tbl, P3, YO, P2 tog tbl; rep from * across to last st, K1 tbl.

Rows 19, 21, 23 and 25: * K1 tbl, P5; rep from * across to last st, K1 tbl.

Row 26: * P1 tbl, K5; rep from * across to last st, P1 tbl.
Rep Row 1-26 for Lace Pattern.

Note: 2 selvedge sts are worked each side on all non-shaping rows as follows:
RS Rows: K1, K1 tbl, work across to last 2 sts, K1 tbl, K1.
WS Rows: P1, P1 tbl, work across to last 2 sts, P1 tbl, P1.

REVERSE STOCKINETTE STITCH (Rev St st): Any number of sts

Purl RS rows, knit WS rows.

BACK

Cast on 87{99-111-123} sts.

Establish Patterns (RS): K1, (K1 tbl, P5) 1{2-3-4} time(s), place marker (PM) **(see Markers, page 121)**, work Row 1 of Lace Pattern over center 73 sts, PM, (P5, K1 tbl) 1{2-3-4} time(s), K1.

WS Row: P1, (P1 tbl, K5) 1{2-3-4} time(s), work Row 2 of Lace Pattern over center 73 sts, (K5, P1 tbl) 1{2-3-4} time(s), P1.

Work as established until 26 rows of Lace Pattern have been worked 3 times [approximately 12" (30.5 cm)].

Discontinue Lace Pattern, but continue all twisted sts, working remaining sts in Rev St st. Work until piece measures 14" (35.5 cm), end WS.

Instructions continued on page 74.

Armhole Shaping (RS):

Bind off 3 sts at the beginning of the next 2{2-2-4} rows, then 2 sts at the beginning of the next 2{4-4-4} rows — 77{85-97-103} sts.

Next (decrease) Row (RS):

K1, SSK, work across to last 3 sts, K2 tog, K1: 75{83-95-101} sts.

Rep decrease row every RS row 5{6-9-9} times — 65{71-77-83} sts.

Work as established until Armholes measure 7{7$\frac{1}{2}$-8-8$\frac{1}{2}$}"/ 18{19-20.5-21.5} cm, end WS.

Back Neck and Shoulder Shaping (RS):

Mark center 33 sts. Bind off 2{3-4-5} sts, work to center marker; join second ball of yarn and bind off center 33 sts, work to end.

Bind off 2{3-4-5} sts at the beginning of the next 5 rows AND AT THE SAME TIME, bind off at each Neck edge 5 sts twice.

LEFT FRONT

Cast on 45{51-57-63} sts.

Establish Patterns (RS):

K1, (K1 tbl, P5) 1{2-3-4} time(s), PM, work Row 1 of Lace Pattern over next 37 sts, K1.

WS Row:

P1, work Row 2 of Lace Pattern over 37 sts, (K5, P1 tbl) 1{2-3-4} time(s), P1.

Work as established until 26 rows of Lace Pattern have been worked 3 times [approximately 12" (30.5 cm)].

Discontinue Lace Pattern, but continue all twisted sts, working remaining sts in Rev St st. Work until piece measures 14" (35.5 cm), end WS.

Armhole Shaping (RS):

Bind off 3 sts at the beginning of the next 1{1-1-2} RS row(s), then 2 sts at the beginning of the next 1{2-2-2} RS row(s) — 40{44-50-53} sts.

Next (decrease) Row (RS):

K1, SSK, work across — 39{43-49-52} sts.

Rep decrease row every RS row 5{6-9-9} times AND AT THE SAME TIME, when Armhole measures 2$\frac{1}{2}${3-3$\frac{1}{2}$-4}"/ 6.5{7.5-9-10} cm, end RS and begin Neck Shaping.

Front Neck Shaping (WS):

Continue Armhole shaping if necessary and bind off 8 sts at beginning of row.

Continue to bind off at Neck edge 4 sts once, 3 sts once, then 2 sts twice.

Next (decrease) Row (RS):

Work across to last 3 sts, K2 tog, K1.

Rep decrease row ever RS row 8 times — 6{9-12-15} sts.

When Armhole measures 7{7$\frac{1}{2}$-8-8$\frac{1}{2}$}"/ 18{19-20.5-21.5} cm, end WS.

Shoulder Shaping (RS):

Bind off 2{3-4-5} sts at the beginning of the next 3 RS rows.

RIGHT FRONT

Cast on 45{51-57-63} sts.

Establish Patterns (RS):

K1, work Row 1 of Lace Pattern over next 37 sts, PM, (P5, K1 tbl) 1{2-3-4} time(s), K1.

Complete as for Left Front, reversing all shaping.

SLEEVES

Cast on 67{67-71-75} sts.

Establish Patterns (RS):

K1, K1 tbl, P 13{13-15-17}, PM, work Row 1 of Lace Pattern over next 37 sts, PM, P 13{13-15-17}, K1 tbl, K1.

WS Row:

P1, P1 tbl, K 13{13-15-17}, work Row 2 of Lace Pattern over 37 sts, K 13{13-15-17}, P1 tbl, P1.

Work as established until 26 rows of Lace Pattern are complete.

Discontinue Lace Pattern, but continue all twisted sts, working remaining sts in Rev St st.

Work until piece measures 6$\frac{1}{2}$" (16.5 cm), end WS.

Cap Shaping (RS):

Bind off 3 sts at the beginning of the next 2 rows, then 2 sts at the beginning of the next 2 rows — 57{57-61-65} sts.

Next (decrease) Row (RS):
K1, SSK, work across to last 3 sts, K2 tog, K1 — 55{55-59-63} sts.

Rep decrease row (alternately every 4th and 2nd row) 4{5-5-5} times, then every 4th row 1{0-0-0} time(s), *(see Zeros, page 121)*, then every RS row 0{1-1-3} time(s) — 37{33-37-37} sts.

Bind off 2{0-2-2} sts at the beginning of the next 2 rows — 33 sts.

Bind off remaining 33 sts.

FINISHING

Sew Fronts to Back at shoulders. Sew side and Sleeve seams *(Fig. 16, page 127)*. Sew Sleeves into armholes, easing in fullness at Cap.

Neck Finishing: With RS facing and smaller needles, pick up 33 sts along Right Front Neck edge to shoulder *(Figs. 15a & b, page 127)*, 45 sts along Back Neck edge, then 33 sts along Left Front Neck edge — 111 sts.

Knit 3 rows.

Bind off all sts in knit.

Left Front Band: With RS facing and smaller needles, pick up 73{76-79-82} sts along Left Front edge.

Knit 3 rows.

Bind off all sts in knit.

Right Front Band: With RS facing and smaller needles, pick up 73{76-79-82} sts along Right Front edge.

Next (buttonhole) Row (WS):
K3, work 3-st buttonhole (by binding off 3 sts and casting on 3 sts while working bind off row), (K 10, work 3-st buttonhole) 2 times, knit across.

Complete as for Left Front Band.

Sew buttons opposite buttonholes. ✳

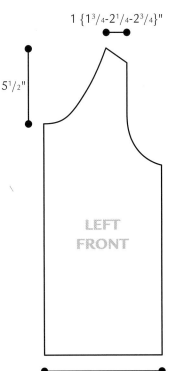

1 {1³/₄-2¹/₄-2³/₄}"

5¹/₂"

LEFT FRONT

8 {9¹/₂-10¹/₂-11¹/₂}"

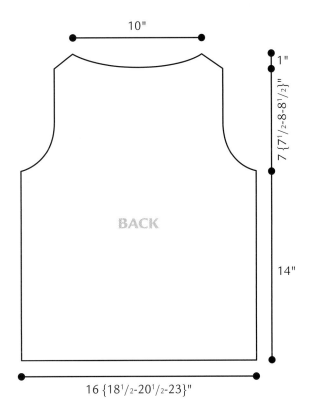

10"

1"

7 {7¹/₂-8-8¹/₂}"

BACK

14"

16 {18¹/₂-20¹/₂-23}"

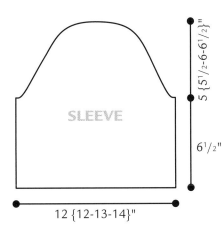

5 {5¹/₂-6-6¹/₂}"

SLEEVE

6¹/₂"

12 {12-13-14}"

75

TUNIC

◼◼◼◻ **INTERMEDIATE**

SIZES
To fit sizes Small {Medium-Large-Extra Large}
Sample in size Small.

MESUREMENTS
Finished bust at underarm: 39{42-46-50}"/99{106.5-117-127} cm
Length to shoulder: 31{31¹/₂-32-32¹/₂}"/78.5{80-81.5-82.5} cm
Version 2: Sleeve width at upper arm: 14{16-16-18}"/35.5{40.5-40.5-45.5} cm

Size Note: Instructions are written for size Small with sizes Medium, Large and
X-Large in braces { }. Instructions will be easier to read if you circle all the numbers
pertaining to your size. If only one number is given, it applies to all sizes.

✳ ✳ ✳ ✳ ✳ ✳ ✳ ✳ ✳ ✳ ✳ ✳ ✳ ✳ ✳ ✳ ✳

In CREATIVE FOCUS LINEN yarn from Nashua Handknits
VERSION #1: Striped
VERSION #2: Solid White
I made the striped version of this cardigan tunic first, inspired by the colors I recall from my many
visits to see family in Oregon. The dark blue running water of the strong rivers, the spring green
of the newly-leafed pear trees in the Rogue River Valley, the natural linen color of dusty sagebrush
in the Cascades, the blue of the vast sky. As accent, I used two different bakelite buttons that I
found in a shop in a tiny cowboy town — one bandana red, the other ranch-denim blue.

When this sweater was in the making, I though how casual it looked, and I wondered if I could
make it look completely different. So I searched for the opposite extreme, as you can see in the
all-white version that has clear antique glass buttons. If the striped one could be worn with dusty
cowboy boots — the other would be fine for a bride at a casual New England wedding!

Both are knitted in the same yarn, half linen, half cotton. The crisp quality of the linen is softened
and lightened by the cotton, and the pattern stitches show full and rich, rather than stringy,
something that could happen with 100% linen.

Instructions begin on page 78.

MATERIALS
NASHUA HANDKNITS
"Creative Focus
Linen" 🔘**4**
(50% Linen, 50% Cotton;
100 grams/220 yards)
Version 1, Striped:
A: Color #200
(Natural):
3{3-3-3} hanks
B: Color #538 (Leaf):
2{2-2-3} hanks
C: Color #4120
(Sky Blue): 1 hank
D: Color #4044
(Light Navy): 1 hank
Version 2, Solid:
Color #100 (Bleached
White): 6{6-7-7} hanks
Straight knitting needles,
sizes 6 (4 mm) **and**
8 (5 mm) **or** sizes
needed to obtain gauge
Stitch markers
Version 1: 3/4" (19 mm)
Buttons - 5 red and
5 blue
Version 2: 3/4" (19 mm)
Buttons - 10

GAUGE

Over Textured Rib using
larger needles: 21 sts and
26 rows = 4" (10 cm)
Over 24 st Lace Panel using
larger needles:
4 3/4" (12 cm) wide
Take time to save time,
check your gauge.

Techniques used:

• K1 tbl *(Fig. 12, page 126)*
• YO *(Figs. 2a & b, page 122)*
• K2 tog *(Fig. 4, page 123)*
• SSK *(Figs. 7a-c, page 124)*
• P2 tog *(Fig. 5, page 123)*
• P2 tog tbl *(Fig. 6, page 124)*

PATTERN STITCHES
STOCKINETTE STITCH
(St st): Any number of sts
Knit RS rows, purl WS rows.

REVERSE STOCKINETTE
STITCH (Rev St st):
Any number of sts
Purl RS rows, knit WS rows.

GARTER RIB: Multiple of
10 sts plus 5
Rows 1, 3 and 5 (RS): P2, K1,
P2, * K5, P2, K1, P2; rep from *
across.
Rows 2 and 4: K5, * P5, K5;
rep from * across.
Row 6: Knit across.
Rep Rows 1-6 for Garter Rib.

TEXTURED RIB: Multiple of
5 sts plus 1
Row 1 (RS): K1 tbl, * P1, K2,
P1, K1 tbl; rep from * across.
Row 2: P1, * K1, P2, K1, P1;
rep from * across.
Row 3: K1 tbl, * P4, K1 tbl; rep
from * across.
Row 4: P1, * K4, P1; rep from *
across.
Repeat Rows 1-4 for Textured
Rib.

LACE PANEL: Panel of 24 sts
(St count varies from row to
row)
Row 1 (RS): P1, K2, YO, SSK,
P1, K4, K2 tog, YO, SSK, K4, P1,
K2, YO, SSK, P1 — 23 sts.
Row 2: K1, P2, YO, P2 tog,
K1, P3, P2 tog tbl, drop YO of
previous row off needle, (YO)
twice, P2 tog, P3, K1, P2, YO,
P2 tog, K1 — 22 sts.
Row 3: P1, K2, YO, SSK, P1,
K2, K2 tog, drop the YO's of the
previous row off needle, (YO) 3
times, SSK, K2, P1, K2, YO, SSK,
P1 — 21 sts.

Row 4: K1, P2, YO, P2 tog, K1,
P1, P2 tog tbl, drop the YO's
of the previous row off needle,
(YO) 4 times, P2 tog, P1, K1,
P2, YO, P2 tog, K1 — 20 sts.
Row 5: P1, K2, YO, SSK, P1,
K2 tog, drop the YO's of the
previous row off needle, then
cast on 4 sts (use backward
loop) on the RH needle
(Fig. 1, page 121), K1 (under
the 4 loose strands of the
dropped YO's), YO and K1
(under the 4 loose strands), cast
on 4 sts (use backward loop) on
the RH needle, SSK, P1, K2, YO,
SSK, P1 — 25 sts.
Row 6: K1, P2, YO, P2 tog, K1,
P5, P2 tog (st and following
YO), P6, K1, P2, YO, P2 tog, K1
— 24 sts.
Rep Rows 1-6 for Lace Panel.

*Note: Version #1 is worked in
Striped Pattern, version #2 is
worked in solid White.*

BACK
Lower Rib Striped Sequence,
Version 1: 12 rows A, 2 rows C,
10 rows A, 2 rows D, 11 rows A.

With larger needles and A
or White, cast on
128{138-148-158} sts.

Begin Lower Rib (and Striped
Sequence for Version 1).

K2 (edge sts), place marker (PM) **(see Markers, page 121)**, work Row 1 of Garter Rib over 35{40-45-50} sts, PM, work Row 1 of Lace Panel over 24 sts, PM, work Row 1 of Textured Rib over center 6 sts, PM, work Row 1 of Lace Panel over 24 sts, PM, work Row 2 of Garter Rib over 35{40-45-50} sts, PM, K2 (edge sts).

Keeping 2 edge sts each side in St st, and continuing pattern and Striped Sequence, work until 36 rows have been completed.

Next (decrease) Row (WS):
P2 (edge sts), P 35{40-45-50} sts and at the same time decrease 4 sts evenly spaced to next marker **(see Increasing or Decreasing Evenly Across A Row, page 123)**, continue Lace Panel over 24 sts as established, continue Textured Rib over center 6 sts, continue Lace Panel over 24 sts as established, P 35{40-45-50} sts and at the same time decrease 4 sts evenly spaced to next marker, P2 — 120{130-140-150} sts.

Rib measures approximately 5" (12.5 cm).

Body Striped Sequence, Version 1: 12 rows B, * 6 rows C, 12 rows A, 6 rows D, 6 rows A, 12 rows B, 6 rows C, 12 rows A, 6 rows D, 12 rows B, 6 rows A; rep from * to end of piece.

Instructions continued on page 80.

Begin Body (Striped Sequence):
Establish Patterns (RS):
K2 (edge sts), work Row 1 of Textured Rib over 31{36-41-46} sts, continue Lace Panel over 24 sts as established, continue Textured Rib over center 6 sts, continue Lace Panel over 24 sts as established, work Row 1 of Textured Rib over 31{36-41-46} sts, K2 (edge sts).

Work even until 16 rows have been completed.

Next (decrease) Row (RS):
K2 (edge sts), P2 tog tbl, work to last 2 sts in this Textured Rib section, then P2 tog, continue Lace Panel over 24 sts, continue Textured Rib over center 6 sts, continue Lace Panel over 24 sts as established, P2 tog tbl, work to last 2 sts in this Textured Rib section, then P2 tog, K2 (edge sts) — 116{126-136-146} sts.

Keeping in patterns as established, work decrease row every 16th row 4 times more — 100{110-120-130} sts.

Keeping in pattern as established, and Striped Sequence, work even until piece measures 23^1/$_2$" (59.5 cm), end WS.

Armhole Shaping (RS):
Bind off 5 sts at the beginning of the next 2 rows, then 0{0-2-2} sts at the beginning of the next 2 rows **(see Zeros, page 121)** — 90{100-106-116} sts.

Next (decrease) Row (RS):
K1, SSK, work across to last 3 sts, K2 tog, K1 — 88{98-104-114} sts.

WS Rows: P2, work as established across to last 2 sts, P2.

Keeping in patterns, rep decrease row every RS row 7{10-11-13} times more — 74{78-82-88} sts.

Work even until Armholes measure 5^1/$_2${6-6^1/$_2$-7}"/ 14{15-16.5-18} cm, end WS.

Back Neck Shaping (RS):
Mark center 48{48-50-50} sts. Work to center marker; join a second ball of yarn and bind off center 48{48-50-50} sts, work to end — 13{15-16-19} sts each side.

Work even as established until Armholes measure 7^1/$_2${8-8^1/$_2$-9}"/ 19{20.5-21.5-23} cm, end WS.

Shoulder Shaping (RS):
Bind off from each shoulder 4{5-5-6} sts twice, then 5{5-6-7} sts once.

LEFT FRONT

With larger needles and A or White, cast on 63{68-73-78} sts.

Begin Lower Rib (and Striped Sequence for Version 1).

Establish Patterns (RS):
K2 (edge sts), PM, work Row 1 of Garter Rib over 35{40-45-50} sts, PM, work Row 1 of Lace Panel over 24 sts, PM, K2 (edge sts).

Keeping 2 edge sts each side in St st, and continuing in pattern and Striped Sequence, work until 36 rows have been completed.

Next (decrease) Row (RS):
P2 (edge sts), continue in Lace Panel over 24 sts as established, P 35{40-45-50} sts and at the same time decrease 4 sts evenly spaced to next marker, P2 (edge sts) — 59{64-69-74} sts.

Rib measures approximately 5" (12.5 cm).

Begin Body (Striped Sequence):
Next Row (RS): K2 (edge sts), work Row 1 of Textured Rib over 31{36-41-46} sts, continue Lace Panel over 24 sts as established, K2 (edge sts).

Work even for 15 more rows, end WS.

Next (decrease) Row (RS):
K2 (edge sts), P2 tog tbl, work to last 2 sts in Textured Rib section, then P2 tog, work Lace Panel over 24 sts as established, K2 (edge sts) — 57{62-67-72} sts.

Keeping in patterns as established, work decrease row every 16th row 4 times more — 49{54-59-64} sts.

Work even until piece measures 23$\frac{1}{2}$" (59.5 cm), end WS.

Armhole Shaping (RS):

Bind off 5 sts at the beginning of the row, then 0{0-2-2} sts at the beginning of the next RS row — 44{49-52-57} sts.

Next (decrease) Row (RS):

K1, SSK, work to end — 43{48-51-56} sts.

WS Rows: P2, work as established across to last 2 sts, P2.

Rep decrease row every RS row 7{10-11-13} times more AND AT THE SAME TIME, continue until Armholes measure 3$\frac{1}{2}${4-4$\frac{1}{2}$-5}"/ 9{10-11.5-12.5} cm, end RS — 36{38-40-43} sts.

Front Neck Shaping (WS):

Bind off 23{23-24-24} sts, work to end — 13{15-16-19} sts.

Work as established until Armholes measure 7$\frac{1}{2}${8-8$\frac{1}{2}$-9}"/ 19{20.5-21.5-23} cm, end WS.

Shoulder Shaping (RS):

Bind off from shoulder 4{5-5-6} sts twice, then 5{5-6-7} sts once.

RIGHT FRONT

With larger needles and A or White, cast on 63{68-73-78} sts. Begin Lower Rib (and Striped Sequence for Version 1).

Instructions continued on page 82.

Establish Patterns (RS):

K2 (edge sts), PM, work Row 1 of Lace Panel over 24 sts, PM, work Row 1 of Garter Rib over 35{40-45-50} sts, PM, K2 (edge sts).

Continue in patterns as established and complete as for Left Front, reversing all shaping.

SLEEVES (Version 2)

With larger needles, cast on 79{89-89-99} sts.

Establish Patterns (RS):

K2 (edge sts), work Row 1 of Garter Rib over center 75{85-85-95} sts, K2 (edge sts).

Keeping 2 edge sts each side in St st, work until piece measures 1¹/₂" (4 cm), end WS.

Cap Shaping (RS): Bind off

6 sts at the beginning of the next 2 rows — 67{77-77-87} sts.

Next (decrease) Row (RS):

K1, SSK, work across to last 3 sts, K2 tog, K1 — 65{75-75-85} sts.

WS Rows: P2, work to last

2 sts, P2.

Rep decrease row every RS row 16{18-19-20} times more — 33{39-37-45} sts.

Bind off 2 sts at the beginning of the next 0{0-2-2} rows, then 3 sts at the beginning of the next 2{4-2-4} rows — 27{27-27-29} sts.

Bind off remaining sts.

FINISHING (Version 1)

Sew Fronts to Back at shoulders.

Armhole Trim: With smaller needles, RS facing and A, pick up 74{80-86-92} sts evenly around armhole edge *(Figs. 15a & b, page 127)*.

Knit 4 rows, change to C and knit 1 row.

Bind off all sts in knit.

Rep for second Armhole.

Sew side seams, including edge *(Fig. 16, page 127)*.

Neck Trim: With smaller needles, RS facing and C, pick up 21{21-22-22} sts along Right Front lower Neck, PM, 18 sts to shoulder, 10 sts to Back Neck, PM, 40{40-42-42} sts along Back Neck edge, PM, 10 sts to shoulder, 18 sts to Left Front lower Neck, PM, 21{21-22-22} sts to end of Left Front lower Neck edge — 138{138-142-142} sts.

Knit every row AND AT THE SAME TIME, on RS rows, K2 tog in the 2 sts before each marker, and SSK in the 2 sts after each marker, in this color sequence: 2 Rows C, 4 rows A, 2 rows B, 1 row D.

Bind off remaining sts in knit.

Left Front Button Band:

With smaller needles, RS facing and D, pick up 130{132-134-136} sts along Left Front edge.

Change to B and knit 4 rows, K2 rows A, then K2 rows C.

Bind off all sts in knit.

Right Front Buttonhole Band: Work same as for Left Band until 2 rows are completed.

Note: There are two different buttonhole types to accommodate different size button.

Next (buttonhole) Row (WS): K2, [work 3-st buttonhole (by binding off 3 sts and casting on 3 sts while working bind off row), K6, K2 tog, YO, SSK, K6] until 9 buttonholes are complete, then knit to end.

Next Row: Knit, working (K1, P1) into each YO of the previous row.

Complete as for Left Front Button Band.

Sew buttons, with blue at top, alternating colors, opposite buttonholes.

FINISHING (Version 2)

Sew Fronts to Back at shoulders and sides *(Fig. 16, page 127)*. Sew Sleeve seams. Sew Sleeves in armholes, easing in fullness at top of Cap.

With smaller needles and RS facing, pick up 21{21-22-22} sts along Right Front lower Neck **(Figs. 15a & b, page 127)**, PM, 18 sts to shoulder, 10 sts to Back Neck, PM, 40{40-42-42} sts along Back Neck edge, PM, 10 sts to shoulder, 18 sts to Left Front lower Neck, PM, 21{21-22-22} sts to end of Left Front lower Neck edge — 138{138-142-142} sts.

Knit every row until Neck Trim measures 1" (2.5 cm) AND AT THE SAME TIME, on RS rows, work K2 tog in the 2 sts before each marker, and SSK in the 2 sts after each marker.

Bind off all remaining sts in knit.

With smaller needles and RS facing, pick up 130{132-134-136} sts along Left Front edge.

Knit 5 rows.

Bind off all sts in knit.

With smaller needles and RS facing, pick up 130{132-134-136} sts along Right Front edge.

K3, work 3-st buttonhole (by binding off 3 sts and casting on 3 sts while working bind off row), (K8, work 3-st buttonhole) 9 times, then knit to end.

Complete as for Left Front Button Band.

Sew button opposite buttonholes. ✤

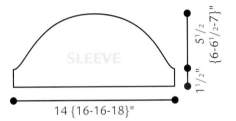

SLEEVE

$5^1/_2$ {6-$6^1/_2$-7}"

$1^1/_2$"

14 {16-16-18}"

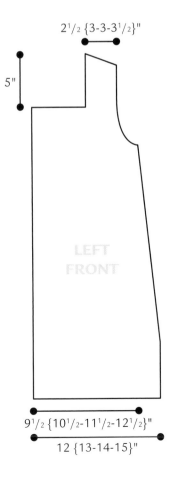

$2^1/_2$ {3-3-$3^1/_2$}"

5"

LEFT FRONT

$9^1/_2$ {$10^1/_2$-$11^1/_2$-$12^1/_2$}"

12 {13-14-15}"

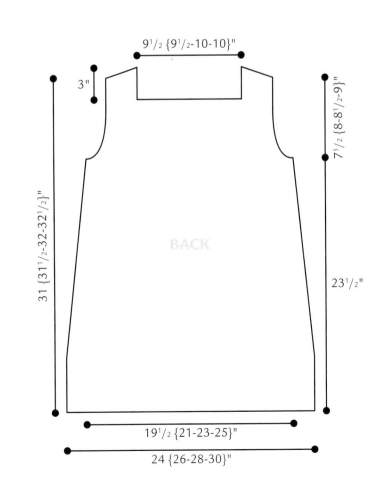

$9^1/_2$ {$9^1/_2$-10-10}"

3"

$7^1/_2$ {8-$8^1/_2$-9}"

31 {$31^1/_2$-32-$32^1/_2$}"

BACK

$23^1/_2$"

$19^1/_2$ {21-23-25}"

24 {26-28-30}"

Versaille
VACATION

◖◕◖◖▱ INTERMEDIATE

SIZES
To fit sizes Small {Medium-Large}
Sample in size Small.

MEASUREMENTS
Lower edge width, buttoned: approximately 26$\frac{1}{2}${28$\frac{1}{2}$-30$\frac{1}{2}$}"/67.5{72.5-77.5} cm
Length to back neck: 13$\frac{1}{2}${14$\frac{1}{2}$-15$\frac{1}{2}$}"/34.5{37-39.5} cm

Size Note: Instructions are written for size Small with sizes Medium and Large in braces
{ }. Instructions will be easier to read if you circle all the numbers pertaining to your
size. If only one number is given, it applies to all sizes.

✳ ✳ ✳ ✳ ✳ ✳ ✳ ✳ ✳ ✳ ✳ ✳ ✳ ✳ ✳ ✳ ✳ ✳

In WICK from Knit One Crochet Too
This shrug was inspired by the little jackets of the 30's and 40's and started with a rough sketch — which
at first I didn't know how to execute! Sometimes I will draw something that looks interesting and then
work my way to understanding how it might be made — an engaging way to work.

Of all the garments in this collection, perhaps this has the most intriguing shape — see the schematic on
page 89. My original sketch showed a fitted piece that was bordered in lace.

Before I could add lace, I had to design a shaped body section, which I did in an interesting way —
starting with the back at the upper shoulders, and narrowing to the lower edge. I incorporated eyelets in
the ribbing, both for lightness and texture. The fronts are picked up along the shoulders of the back and
worked downward too. Then the stitches for the lace borders, which form a sleeve-effect, were picked up
and worked to the sides.

I turned to my all-time favorite lace border from the famous SECOND TREASURY OF KNITTING
PATTERNS by Barbara Walker. She gives this pattern a royal name — VERSAILLE LACE. It is one of the
rare knitted laces that has "yarn-over" elements on both the right side and wrong side rows. The resulting
pattern is rich in depth and texture, and when I tried a yarn which was a mix of soy and polypropylene, it
emphasized those qualities. With a sheen, this tubular strand creates drape without being heavy.

I can picture roaming the acres of gardens at Versaille in the evening, wearing this little coverup....
someday!

Instructions begin on page 86.

KNIT ONE CROCHET TOO "Wick" MEDIUM 4
(53% Soy,
47% Polypropylene;
50 grams/120 yards)
Color #676 (Ocean):
7{7-8} balls
Straight knitting needles,
size 9 (5.5 mm) **or** size
needed to obtain gauge
24" (61 cm) Circular
knitting needle, size 8
(5 mm)
2" (5 cm) Button

GAUGE

Over St st: 20 sts and
27 rows = 4" (10 cm)
Over Wide Eyelet Rib: 22 sts
and 27 rows = 4" (10 cm)
Over Lace Border: 20 sts and
27 rows = 4" (10 cm)
Take time to save time,
check your gauge.

Techniques used:

- YO *(Figs. 2a & b, page 122)*
- K2 tog *(Fig. 4, page 123)*
- P2 tog *(Fig. 5, page 123)*
- P2 tog tbl *(Fig. 6, page 124)*
- SSK *(Figs. 7a-c, page 124)*
- Slip 1 as if to **knit**, K2 tog, PSSO *(Figs. 9a & b, page 125)*

PATTERN STITCHES
STOCKINETTE STITCH
(St st): Any number of sts
Knit RS rows, purl WS rows.

WIDE EYELET RIB: Multiple of 5 sts plus 4

Rows 1, 3, 5 and 7 (RS): P4, * K1, P4; rep from * across.
Rows 2, 4 and 6: K4, * P1, K4; rep from * across.
Row 8: K2, YO, K2 tog, * P1, K2, YO, K2 tog; rep from * across.
Rep Row 1-8 for Wide Eyelet Rib.

NARROW EYELET RIB: Multiple of 4 sts plus 3

Rows 1, 3, 5 and 7 (RS): P3, * K1, P3; rep from * across.
Rows 2, 4 and 6: K3, * P1, K3; rep from * across.
Row 8: K1, YO, K2 tog, * P1, K1, YO, K2 tog; rep from * across.
Rep Rows 1-8 for Narrow Eyelet Rib.

LACE BORDER: Multiple of 10 sts plus 4

Row 1 (WS): Purl across.
Row 2: K2, * YO, SSK, K8; rep from * across to last 2 sts, K2.
Row 3: P2, * YO, P2 tog, P5, P2 tog tbl, YO, P1; rep from * across to last 2 sts, P2.
Row 4: K4, * YO, SSK, K3, K2 tog, YO, K3; rep from * across.
Row 5: P4, * YO, P2 tog, P1, P2 tog tbl, YO, P5; rep from * across.
Row 6: K6, * YO, slip 1, K2 tog, PSSO, YO, K7; rep from * across, end last rep K5.
Row 7: P2, * P3, P2 tog tbl, YO; rep from * across to last 2 sts, P2.
Row 8: K3, * YO, SSK, K3; rep from * across to last st, K1.
Row 9: P3, * P2 tog tbl, YO, P3; rep from * across to last st, P1.
Row 10: K5, * YO, SSK, K3; rep from * across, end last rep K2.
Row 11: P1, * P2 tog tbl, YO, P3; rep from * across to last 3 sts, P3.
Row 12: K2, * YO, SSK, K3; rep from * across to last 2 sts, K2.
Rows 13, 14, 15 and 16: Rep Rows 3, 4, 5 and 6.
Row 17: P3, * P3, YO, P2 tog; rep from * across to last st, P1.
Row 18: K5, * K2 tog, YO, K3; rep from * across, end last rep K2.
Row 19: P3, * YO, P2 tog, P3; rep from * across to last st, P1.
Row 20: K3, * K2 tog, YO, K3; rep from * across to last st, K1.
Row 21: P2, * P3, YO, P2 tog; rep from * across to last 2 sts, P2.
Row 22: K1, * K2 tog, YO, K3; rep from * across to last 3 sts, K3.
Rows 23, 24, 25 and 26: Rep Rows 3, 4, 5 and 6.
Row 27: Purl across.

NOTES

Shrug starts with the Back piece and begins at shoulder/back neck edge and is worked down to the lower edge, gradually narrowing.
Fronts are picked up separately at the Back shoulder and worked down, gradually narrowing.
Stitches for Lace borders are picked up on each side of the joined front and back side edges and worked outwards.

BACK

Cast on 88{98-108} sts.

Establish Patterns (WS):
P2 (edge sts), K4, * P1, K4;
rep from * across to last 2 sts,
P2 (edge sts).

Next Row (RS): Keeping
2 edge sts each side in St st,
work Row 1 of Wide Eyelet Rib
over center 84{94-104} sts,
end K2.

Work in Wide Eyelet Rib until
piece measures approximately
7" (18 cm), ending with Row 7
of pattern.

Next (decrease) Row (WS):
P2, K2 tog, YO, K2 tog, * P1,
K2 tog, YO, K2 tog; rep from *
across to last 2 sts, P2 —
71{79-87} sts.

Next Row (RS): K2, work
Row 1 of Narrow Eyelet Rib over
67{75-83} sts to last 2 sts, K2.

Work in Narrow Eyelet Rib until
piece measures 10" (25.5 cm),
end RS.

Next (decrease) Row (WS):
P2, K1, K2 tog, * P1, K1, K2 tog;
rep from * across to last 2 sts,
P2 — 54{60-66} sts.

Next Row (RS): K2, P2, * K1,
P2; rep from * across to last
2 sts, K2.

Work in Rib as established
until Back piece measures
12¹/₂" (32 cm), end RS row.

Instructions continued on page 88.

Instructions continued on page 88.

Next (decrease) Row (WS): P2, K2 tog, * P1, K2 tog; rep from * across to last 2 sts, P2 — 37{41-45} sts.

Next Row (RS): K2, P1, * K1, P1; rep from * across to last 2 sts, K2.

Work in Rib as established until piece measures 13$\frac{1}{2}${14$\frac{1}{2}$-15$\frac{1}{2}$}"/ 34.5{37-39.5} cm.

Bind off all sts.

RIGHT FRONT

With RS of Back Neck facing, beginning at right outer edge, pick up 28{33-38} sts **(Figs. 15a & b, page 127)**, 1 st in each of the first 28{33-38} sts of back piece.

Establish Patterns (WS): P2 (edge sts), K4, * P1, K4; rep from * across to last 2 sts, P2 (edge sts).

Next Row (RS): Keeping 2 edge sts each side in St st, work Row 1 of Wide Eyelet Rib over center 24{29-34} sts, end K2.

Work even in Wide Eyelet Rib until piece measures approximately 7" (18 cm), ending with Row 7 of pattern.

Next (decrease) Row (WS): P2, K2 tog, YO, K2 tog, * P1, K2 tog, YO, K2 tog; rep from * across to last 2 sts, P2 — 23{27-31} sts.

Next Row (RS): K2, work Row 1 of Narrow Eyelet Rib over 19{23-27} sts, K2.

Work in Narrow Eyelet Rib until piece measures 10" (25.5 cm), end RS.

Next (decrease) Row (WS): P2, K1, K2 tog, * P1, K1, K2 tog; rep from * across to last 2 sts, P2 — 18{21-24} sts.

Next Row (RS): K2, P2, * K1, P2; rep from * across to last 2 sts, K2.

Work in Rib as established until piece measures 12$\frac{1}{2}$" (32 cm), end RS.

Next (decrease) Row (WS): P2, K2 tog, * P1, K2 tog; rep from * across to last 2 sts, P2 — 13{15-17} sts.

Next Row (RS): K2, P1, * K1, P1; rep from * across to last 2 sts, K2.

Work in Rib as established until piece measures 13$\frac{1}{2}${14$\frac{1}{2}$-15$\frac{1}{2}$}"/ 34.5{37-39.5} cm.

Bind off all sts.

LEFT FRONT

Work same as for Right Front, begin picking up sts in the 28th{33rd-38th} st from left edge, picking up toward the outer edge.

RIGHT SIDE LACE BORDER

With RS facing, beginning at lower Back, pick up 110{120-130} sts evenly along side edges of Right Back and Right Front.

Row 1 (WS): P2, K1 (edge sts), knit 104{114-124} sts, K1, P2 (edge sts).

Row 2: K2, P1 (edge sts), knit 104{114-124} sts, P1, K2 (edge sts).

Rep Rows 1 and 2.

Next Row (WS): Keeping 3 edge sts each side as established, work Row 1 of Lace Border over center 104{114-124} sts.

Work even until 27 Lace Border rows are complete.

Row 1 (RS): K2, P1, K 104{114-124}, P1, K2.

Row 2: P2, K1, K 104{114-124}, K1, P2.

Rep Rows 1 and 2, then Row 1 again.

Narrow the Border (WS): Bind off first 10 sts, P1, K1 (edge sts), work Row 1 of Lace Border over 84{94-104} sts, K1, P2 (edge sts), bind off last 10 sts — 90{100-110} sts.

Cut yarn and re-tie at beginning of next RS row.
Work even until 27 Lace Border rows are complete.

Row 1 (RS): K2, P1, K 84{94-104}, P1, K2.

Row 2: P2, K1, K 84{94-104}, K1, P2.

Rep Rows 1 and 2.

Bind off all sts.

LEFT SIDE LACE BORDER

Work as for Right Side Lace Border on Left Front and Left Back side of shrug.

FINISHING

Sew each Front to Back along bound-off 10 sts as side edges. Sew sides of second repeat of lace together on each side to form sleeve.

Front Edge Finishing:

With circular needle and RS facing, starting at lower Right Front, pick up 59{63-67} sts along Right Front edge, 34{37-40} sts along Back Neck edge, then 59{63-67} sts along Left Front edge — 152{163-174} sts.

Knit WS row to last 9 sts, make 5-st buttonhole (by binding off 5 sts and casting on 5 sts while working bind off row), knit to end.

Knit RS row.

Bind off all sts in knit.

Sew button opposite buttonhole. ✳

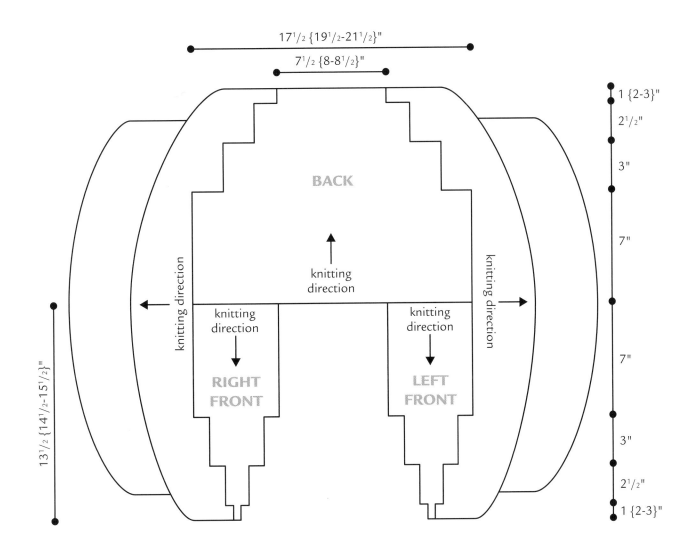

17½ {19½-21½}"

7½ {8-8½}"

BACK

knitting direction

knitting direction

knitting direction

knitting direction

knitting direction

RIGHT FRONT

LEFT FRONT

13½ {14½-15½}"

1 {2-3}"

2½"

3"

7"

7"

3"

2½"

1 {2-3}"

Leaf Dance SHAWL

▬▬▬▭ INTERMEDIATE

SIZE
One size

MEASUREMENTS
Length: Approximately 65" (165 cm)
Width: Approximately 20" (51 cm)

✳   ✳   ✳   ✳   ✳   ✳   ✳   ✳   ✳   ✳   ✳   ✳   ✳   ✳   ✳   ✳   ✳   ✳

In DREAM yarn from Tahki
I had it in my head that I wanted to make an heirloom quality, very dressy summer shawl.
When I found a wonderful fine gauge wool blend, it occurred to me that if I doubled the yarn
I could make a matching tank top (see page 94). One idea often leads to another, if you let it!

I chose a color reminiscent of a couple of my favorite plants that grow in cool shade: Lady's
Mantle and the chartreuse varieties of hosta plants. Both projects share a leaf-patterned lace.

MATERIALS

TAHKI "Dream"
(80% Wool, 20% Nylon;
50 grams/262 yards)
   Color #28 (Chartreuse):
   5 balls
Straight knitting needles,
   size 6 (4 mm) **or** size
   needed to obtain gauge
Stitch markers
T-pins

GAUGE

Over Lace Patterns, after wet
blocking with pins to open
fabric and allowing swatch
to dry thoroughly:
20 sts and 30-32 rows =
4" (10 cm)
Take time to save time,
check your gauge.

Techniques used:
• K1 tbl *(Fig. 12, page 126)*
• YO *(Fig. 2a, page 122)*
• K2 tog *(Fig. 4, page 123)*
• SSK *(Figs. 7a-c, page 124)*
• K3 tog *(Fig. 8, page 124)*
• Slip 1 as if to **knit**, K2 tog,
  PSSO *(Figs. 9a & b,
  page 125)*
• Slip 2 tog as if to **knit**, K1,
  P2SSO *(Figs. 10a & b,
  page 125)*

Instructions begin on page 92.

PATTERN STITCHES
STOCKINETTE STITCH
(St st): Any number of sts
Knit RS rows, purl WS rows.

GARTER STITCH: Any number of sts
Knit every row.

CENTER LACE: Multiple of 22 sts plus 1

Row 1 (RS): K3, * K2 tog, YO, K1 tbl, K2, K2 tog, K1 tbl, YO, K1, YO, K1 tbl, SSK, K2, K1 tbl, YO, SSK, K5; rep from *, end last rep K3.

Row 2 and all WS rows: Purl across.

Row 3: K2, * K2 tog, YO, K1 tbl, K2, K2 tog, K1, K1 tbl, YO, K1, YO, K1 tbl, K1, SSK, K2, K1 tbl, YO, SSK, K3; rep from *, end last rep K2.

Row 5: K1, * K2 tog, YO, K1 tbl, K2, K2 tog, K2, YO, K1 tbl, K1, K1 tbl, YO, K2, SSK, K2, K1 tbl, YO, SSK, K1; rep from * across.

Row 7: K2 tog, * YO, K1 tbl, K2, K2 tog, K2, YO, K1 tbl, K3, K1 tbl, YO, K2, SSK, K2, K1 tbl, YO, slip 1, K2 tog, PSSO; rep from *, end last rep SSK instead of slip 1, K2 tog, PSSO.

Row 9: K1, * YO, K3, K2 tog, K2, YO, SSK, K3, K2 tog, YO, K2, SSK, K3, YO, K1; rep from * across.

Row 11: K1, * YO, K3, SSK, K2, YO, SSK, K3, K2 tog, YO, K2, K2 tog, K3, YO, K1; rep from * across.

Row 13: K1, * K1 tbl, YO, K3, SSK, K1, K1 tbl, YO, SSK, K1, K2 tog, YO, K1 tbl, K1, K2 tog, K3, YO, K1 tbl, K1; rep from * across.

Row 15: K2, * K1 tbl, YO, K3, SSK, K1, K1 tbl, YO, slip 1, K2 tog, PSSO, YO, K1 tbl, K1, K2 tog, K3, YO, K1 tbl, K3; rep from *, end last rep K2.

Row 17: K1, * K2 tog, YO, K1 tbl, YO, K3, K3 tog, YO, K1 tbl, K1, K1 tbl, YO, slip 1, K2 tog, PSSO, K3, YO, K1 tbl, YO, SSK, K1; rep from * across.

Row 19: K2 tog, * YO, K1 tbl, K1, K1 tbl, K2, (K2 tog, YO) 2 times, K1, (YO, SSK) 2 times, K2, K1 tbl, K1, K1 tbl, YO, slip 1, K2 tog, PSSO; rep from *, end last rep SSK instead of slip 1, K2 tog, PSSO.

Row 21: K1, * YO, SSK, K3, K2 tog, YO, K1 tbl, K2 tog, YO, K1, YO, SSK, K1 tbl, YO, SSK, K3, K2 tog, YO, K1; rep from * across.

Row 23: K1, * K1 tbl, YO, SSK, K1, K2 tog, YO, K1 tbl, K1, K2 tog, YO, K1, YO, SSK, K1, K1 tbl, YO, SSK, K1, K2 tog, YO, K1 tbl, K1; rep from * across.

Row 25: K2, * K1 tbl, YO, K3 tog, YO, K1 tbl, K2, K2 tog, YO, K1, YO, SSK, K2, K1 tbl, YO, slip 1, K2 tog, PSSO, YO, K1 tbl, K3; rep from *, end last rep K2.

Row 26 (WS): Purl across.
Rep Row 1-26 for Center Lace.

LEAF LACE PANEL: 23 sts
(St count varies from row to row)

Row 1 (WS) and all other WS rows: Purl across.

Row 2: SSK, YO, slip 2, K1, P2SSO, YO, K1 tbl, YO, SSK, K7, K2 tog, YO, K1 tbl, YO, slip 2, K1, P2SSO, YO, K2 tog — 21 sts.

Row 4: SSK, YO, K1, YO, K3, YO, SSK, K5, K2 tog, YO, K3, YO, K1, YO, K2 tog — 23 sts.

Row 6: K1, (YO, slip 2, K1, P2SSO) 2 times, YO, K1 tbl, YO, SSK, K3, K2 tog, YO, K1 tbl, (YO, slip 2, K1, P2SSO) 2 times, YO, K1 — 21 sts.

Row 8: (K1, YO, K3, YO) 2 times, SSK, K1, K2 tog, (YO, K3, YO, K1) 2 times — 27 sts.

Row 10: SSK, (YO, slip 2, K1, P2SSO) 3 times, YO, K1 tbl, YO, slip 1, K2 tog, PSSO, YO, K1 tbl, (YO, slip 2, K1, P2SSO) 3 times, YO, K2 tog — 21 sts.

Row 12: SSK, YO, K1, YO, K2, K2 tog, YO, K3, YO, K1, YO, K3, YO, SSK, K2, YO, K1, YO, K2 tog — 25 sts.

Row 14: K1, (YO, slip 2, K1, P2SSO) 2 times, YO, K2 tog, K3, YO, K1, YO, K3, SSK, (YO, slip 2, K1, P2SSO) 2 times, YO, K1 — 23 sts.

Row 16: K1, YO, K2, K2 tog, YO, K2 tog, K9, SSK, YO, SSK, K2, YO, K1 — 23 sts.
Rep Rows 1-16 for Leaf Lace Panel.

SHAWL
Center Section:
Cast on 71 sts very loosely.

Knit 10 rows.

Next Row (RS): K2 (edge sts), work Row 1 of Center Lace over 67 sts, K2 (edge sts).

Keeping 2 edge sts each side in St st, work even until 6 reps of pattern (156 rows) are complete, end WS.

Knit 10 rows.

Bind off all sts very loosely in knit.

Left Side Section:
With RS facing, beginning at bound off edge of Center Section, pick up 102 sts *(Figs. 15a & b, page 127)* evenly spaced along side edge (pick up 2 sts in from edge).

Next Row (WS): K5 (edge sts), work Row 1 of Leaf Lace Panel over 92 sts, placing markers between each 23 sts panel *(see Markers, page 121)*, K5 (edge sts).

Keeping 5 edge sts each side in Garter st, work even until 12 rep of pattern (192 rows) are complete, end RS.

Purl WS row. Knit 10 rows.

Bind off all sts very loosely in knit.

Right Side Section:
Work same as for Left Side Section, picking up sts along other edge of Center Section.

FINISHING
Wet in cold water. Squeeze in towels to remove excess moisture. Block with pins on clean cardboard, or carpeted surface covered with a sheet, to the approximately measurement of 65" x 20" (165 cm x 51 cm).

Allow to dry thoroughly. ✳

Leaf Dance TANK TOP

⬛⬛⬛⬜ INTERMEDIATE

SIZES
To fit sizes Small {Medium-Large-Extra Large}
Sample in size Small.

MEASUREMENTS
Finished bust at underarm: 34{37-43-47}"/86.5{94-109-119.5} cm
Finished length to shoulder: 21{21^1/$_2$-22-22^1/$_2$}"/53.5{54.5-56-57} cm

Size Note: Instructions are written for size Small with sizes Medium, Large and X-Large in braces { }. Instructions will be easier to read if you circle all the numbers pertaining to your size. If only one number is given, it applies to all sizes.

❋　❋　❋　❋　❋　❋　❋　❋　❋　❋　❋　❋　❋　❋　❋　❋　❋　❋

In DREAM yarn from Tahki
I designed this tank to be worked in 2 strands of the fine yarn I used for the lace shawl on page 90. By doing this, the lace panel of the tank has a slightly larger scale while still reflecting the pattern in the shawl. And the shaping could not be easier. A little bit of ribbing at each side gives the tank a fitted look without a lot of complex shaping. And the neckline sits nicely without any trim at all.

This is a tank that is not hard to make—a summer staple—and would be nice worked in any yarn that has a little body.

MATERIALS

TAHKI "Dream"
(80% Wool, 20% Nylon;
50 grams/262 yards)
   Color #28 (Chartreuse):
      6{7-8-9} balls
Straight knitting needles,
   size 5 (3.75 mm) **or** size
   needed to obtain gauge
24" (61 cm) Circular
   knitting needle, size 5
   (3.75 mm)
Stitch markers

GAUGE

Over St st with 2 strands
of yarn held together:
24 sts and 30 rows =
4" (10 cm)
Over 23 st Lace Panel with
2 strands of yarn held
together: Approximately
4" (10 cm) wide
Take time to save time,
check your gauge.

Techniques used:

• K1 tbl *(Fig. 12, page 126)*
• YO *(Fig. 2a, page 122)*
• K2 tog *(Fig. 4, page 123)*
• SSK *(Figs. 7a-c, page 124)*
• Slip 2 tog as if to **knit**, K1,
  P2SSO *(Figs. 10a & b,
  page 125)*
• Slip 1 as if to **knit**, K2 tog,
  PSSO *(Figs. 9a & b,
  page 125)*

Instructions begin on page 96.

95

PATTERN STITCHES

K1/P1 RIB: Odd number of sts

Row 1 (RS): K2, P1, * K1, P1; rep from * across to last 2 sts, end K2.

Row 2: P2, K1, * P1, K1; rep from * across to last 2 sts, end P2.

Rep Rows 1 and 2 for K1/P1 Rib.

P3/K3 RIB: Multiple of 6 sts plus 3

Row 1 (RS): P3, * K3, P3; rep from * across.

Row 2: K3, * P3, K3; rep from * across.

Rep Rows 1 and 2 for P3/K3 Rib.

STOCKINETTE STITCH (St st): Any number of sts.

Knit RS rows, purl WS rows.

LACE PANEL: 23 sts (St count varies from row to row)

Row 1 (WS) and all other WS rows: Purl across.

Row 2: SSK, YO, slip 2, K1, P2SSO, YO, K1 tbl, YO, SSK, K7, K2 tog, YO, K1 tbl, YO, slip 2, K1, P2SSO, YO, K2 tog — 21 sts.

Row 4: SSK, YO, K1, YO, K3, YO, SSK, K5, K2 tog, YO, K3, YO, K1, YO, K2 tog — 23 sts.

Row 6: K1, (YO, slip 2, K1, P2SSO) 2 times, YO, K1 tbl, YO, SSK, K3, K2 tog, YO, K1 tbl, (YO, slip 2, K1, P2SSO) 2 times, YO, K1 — 21 sts.

Row 8: (K1, YO, K3, YO) 2 times, SSK, K1, K2 tog, (YO, K3, YO, K1) 2 times — 27 sts.

Row 10: SSK, (YO, slip 2, K1, P2SSO) 3 times, YO, K1 tbl, YO, slip 1, K2 tog, PSSO, YO, K1 tbl, (YO, slip 2, K1, P2SSO) 3 times, YO, K2 tog — 21 sts.

Row 12: SSK, YO, K1, YO, K2, K2 tog, YO, K3, YO, K1, YO, K3, YO, SSK, K2, YO, K1, YO, K2 tog — 25 sts.

Row 14: K1, (YO, slip 2, K1, P2SSO) 2 times, YO, K2 tog, K3, YO, K1, YO, K3, SSK, (YO, slip 2, K1, P2SSO) 2 times, YO, K1 — 23 sts.

Row 16: K1, YO, K2, K2 tog, YO, K2 tog, K9, SSK, YO, SSK, K2, YO, K1 — 23 sts.

Rep Rows 1-16 for Lace Panel.

BACK

With 2 strands of yarn held together, cast on 121{135-161-175} sts.

Work in K1/P1 Rib for 1" (2.5 cm), end RS.

Purl WS row decreasing 10{12-14-16} sts evenly spaced *(see Increasing or Decreasing Evenly Across A Row, page 123)* — 111{123-147-159} sts.

Next Row (RS): K2 (edge sts), place marker (PM) *(see Markers, page 121)*, work Row 1 of P3/K3 Rib over 15{21-33-39} sts, PM, work in St st over 27 sts, PM, work Row 1 of Lace Panel over center 23 sts, PM, work in St st over 27 sts, PM, work Row 1 of P3/K3 Rib over 15{21-33-39} sts, PM, end K2 (edge sts).

Keeping 2 edge sts each side in St st, work even in patterns until piece measures 14" (35.5 cm), end WS.

Armhole Shaping (RS): Bind off 6 sts at the beginning of the next 2 rows, then 0{0-3-3} sts at the beginning of the next 2 rows *(see Zeros, page 121)*.

Next (decrease) Row (RS): K1, SSK, work in patterns as established to last 3 sts, K2 tog, K1.

WS Rows: P2, work as established to last 2 sts, P2.

Rep decreases every RS row 4{7-13-16} times more AND AT THE SAME TIME, when Armholes measure 2½{3-3½-4}"/6.5{7.5-9-10} cm, end with Row 1, 5 or 15 of Lace Panel (WS row) and begin Back Neck Shaping.

Back Neck Shaping (RS):

Continue Armhole Shaping if necessary. Mark center 25 sts. Work across to marker; join a second double strand and bind off center 25 sts, work as established to end.

Working both sides at the same time with separate double strands, work WS row in patterns as established.

Next (decrease) Row (RS):

Work in patterns as established to last 4 sts of first half, K2 tog, K2; on second half, K2, SSK, work as established to end.

Work WS row.

Rep Neck decreases every RS row 13 more times — 19{22-25-28} sts remain each side.

Work even until Armholes measure 7{7^1/$_2$-8-8^1/$_2$}"/ 18{19-20.5-21.5} cm, end WS.

Shoulder Shaping (RS):

Bind off from each shoulder 6{7-8-9} sts twice, then 7{8-9-10} sts once.

FRONT

Work same as Back until Armholes measure 1^1/$_2${2-2^1/$_2$-3}"/4{5-6.5-7.5} cm, end with Row 1, 5 or 15 of Lace Panel (WS row) and begin Front Neck Shaping.

Instructions continued on page 98.

Front Neck Shaping (RS):

Continue Armhole Shaping if necessary. Mark center 25 sts. Work across to center marker; join a second double strand and bind off center 25 sts, work as established to end.

Working both sides at the same time with separate double strands, work WS row in patterns as established.

Next (decrease) Row (RS):

Work in patterns as established to last 4 sts of first half, K2 tog, K2; on second half, K2, SSK, work as established to end.

Work WS row.

Rep Neck decreases every RS row 10 more times, then every 4th row 3 times — 19{22-25-28} sts remain each side.

Work even until Armholes measure 7{7^1/$_2$-8-8^1/$_2$}/ 18{19-20.5-21.5} cm, end WS.

Shoulder Shaping (RS):

Bind off from each shoulder 6{7-8-9} sts twice, then 7{8-9-10} sts once.

FINISHING

Sew Front to Back at shoulders. Sew side seams *(Fig. 16, page 127)*.

Wet block if desired. ✶

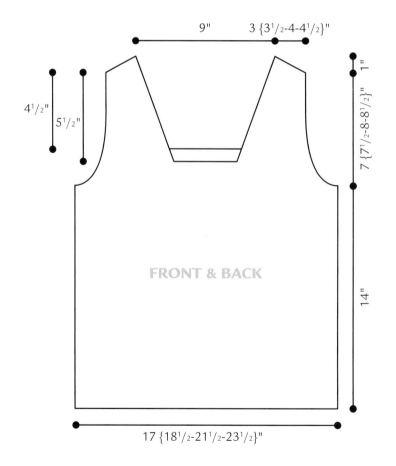

9"   3 {3^1/$_2$-4-4^1/$_2$}"

1"   1"

7{7^1/$_2$-8-8^1/$_2$}"

4^1/$_2$"

5^1/$_2$"

14"

FRONT & BACK

17 {18^1/$_2$-21^1/$_2$-23^1/$_2$}"

Rosebud
TANK TOP

◼◼◼◻ INTERMEDIATE

SIZES

To fit sizes Small {Medium-Large-Extra Large}
Sample in size Small.

MEASUREMENTS

Finished bust at underarm: 34{38-42-46}"/86.5{96.5-106.5-117} cm
Length to shoulder: 23{23^1/$_2$-24-24^1/$_2$}"/58.5{59.5-61-62} cm

Size Note: Instructions are written for size Small with sizes Medium, Large and
X-Large in braces { }. Instructions will be easier to read if you circle all the numbers
pertaining to your size. If only one number is given, it applies to all sizes.

✳ ✳ ✳ ✳ ✳ ✳ ✳ ✳ ✳ ✳ ✳ ✳ ✳ ✳ ✳ ✳ ✳ ✳

In SOJOBAMA from Schulana
This sweater is inspired by my favorite heirloom rose, a pale pink stunner that makes buds into
late fall and whose name I do not know. Inspired, I combined two bud-like patterns, one rib-
like for the lower section, and the other an allover nub on a purl-like background.

With repetitive patterns and simple shaping, this tank is fun to knit. If you like, knit a belt to go
under the bust, close with a shell buckle. Or make a belt of ties made of cords of the same yarn.

This tubular yarn made of bamboo and soy just glows. It also lends the sweater a drapey
quality that is dressy, like silk.

For a more casual tank top, you might choose cotton with a sheen, or linen for a more
dry-feeling fabric. I think this tank would also be great shortened — a midriff-baring top, with
only a couple of repeats of the lower pattern as a slight ribbing.

Instructions begin on page 100.

MATERIALS

SCHULANA
"Sojabama" ⓵ LIGHT 3
(55% Bamboo, 45% Soy;
50 grams/120 yards)
Color #05 (Soft Pink):
7{7-8-9} balls
Straight knitting needles,
size 6 (4 mm) **or** size
needed to obtain gauge
16" (40.5 cm) Circular
needle, size 5 (3.75 mm)
Stitch markers

GAUGE

Over Border Pattern,
slightly stretched:
21 sts and 32 rows =
4"(10 cm)
Over Bud Pattern: 22 sts and
30-32 rows = 4" (10 cm)

Techniques used:

• YO *(Figs. 2a-d, page 122)*
• K2 tog *(Fig. 4, page 123)*
• SSK *(Figs. 7a-c, page 124)*
• K3 tog *(Fig. 8, page 124)*

PATTERN STITCHES
STOCKINETTE STITCH
(St st): Any number of sts
Knit RS rows, purl WS rows.

REVERSE STOCKINETTE STITCH (Rev St st): Any number of sts
Purl RS rows, knit WS rows.

BORDER PATTERN: Multiple of 10 sts plus 4
Note: St count varies from row to row.

Row 1 (WS): P4, * K6, P4;
rep from * across.
Row 2: YO, SSK, K2 tog, YO,
* P2, [(K1, P1 K1) into next st]
twice, P2, YO, SSK, K2 tog, YO;
rep from * across.
Rows 3, 5 and 7: P4, * K2, P6,
K2, P4; rep from * across.
Rows 4 and 6: YO, SSK,
K2 tog, YO, * P2, K6, P2, YO,
SSK, K2 tog, YO; rep from *
across.
Row 8: YO, SSK, K2 tog, YO,
* P2, (K3 tog) twice, P2, YO,
SSK, K2 tog, YO; rep from *
across.
Row 9: P4, * K6, P4; rep from *
across.
Row 10: YO, SSK, K2 tog, YO,
* P6, YO, SSK, K2 tog, YO;
rep from * across.
Rep Row 1-10 for Border
Pattern.

BUD PATTERN: Multiple of 4 sts plus 2
Note: St count varies from row to row.

Twist 3 sts: Insert the RH
needle in front of the third st
from LH needle and knit this
st, slip the first st from the LH
needle knitwise to RH needle,
knit the 2nd st, drop 3rd st
(already knitted in) then pass
the 1st (slipped) st over the 2nd
(knitted) st.

Row 1 (WS): K2, * P2, K2;
rep from * across.
Row 2: P2, * K1, YO, K1, P2;
rep from * across.
Row 3: K2, * P1, K1, P1, K2;
rep from * across.
Rows 4 and 5: Knit the knit
sts and purl the purl sts, as they
present themselves.
Row 6: P2, * Twist 3 sts, P2;
rep from * across.
Row 7: P2, * K2, P2; rep from *
across.
Row 8: K1, YO, K1, * P2, K1,
YO, K1; rep from * across.
Row 9: P1, K1, P1, * K2, P1,
K1, P1; rep from * across.
Rows 10 and 11: Knit the knit
sts and purl the purl sts, as they
present themselves.
Row 12: Twist 3 sts, * P2, Twist
3 sts; rep from * across.
Rep Rows 1-12 for Bud Pattern.

Instructions continued on page 102.

BACK & FRONT

Cast on 92{102-112-122} sts. Knit RS row.

Next Row (WS): P2 (edge sts), place marker (PM) *(see Markers, page 121)*, work 2 sts in Rev St st, PM, work Row 1 of Border Pattern over 84{94-104-114} sts, PM, work 2 sts in Rev St st, PM, P2 (edge sts).

Keeping 2 edge sts in St st, work even in patterns as established until 9 reps of Border Pattern are completed, ending with Row 10 **[piece measures approximately 11¹/₂" (29 cm)]**.

Work Row 1 of Border Pattern again.

Knit RS row increasing 2{4-2-4} sts evenly spaced *(see Increasing or Decreasing Evenly Across A Row, page 123)* — 94{106-114-126} sts.

Next Row (WS): P2 (edge sts), PM, work Row 1 of Bud Pattern over 90{102-110-122} sts, P2 (edge sts).

Work even until piece measures 16" (40.5 cm), end WS.

Shape Armhole (RS): Keeping to pattern, bind off 5 sts at the beginning of the next 2 rows.

Next (decrease) Row (RS): K1, SSK, work in pattern to last 3 sts, K2 tog, K1.

Row 2 (WS): P2, work in pattern to last 2 sts, P2.

Rep decrease row every 2ⁿᵈ row 0{5-5-9} times *(see Zeros, page 121)*, then every 4ᵗʰ row 5{4-6-6} times AND AT THE SAME TIME, when 24{24-36-36} rows of Bud Pattern are complete, begin Neck Shaping.

Neck Shaping (WS): Continue Armhole Shaping if necessary. Mark center 30{30-34-34} sts. P1, work in pattern to center marker; join a second ball of yarn and bind off center 30{30-34-34} sts, work in pattern to last st, P1.

Working both sides at the same time with separate balls of yarn and keeping to pattern, work 2 more rows.

Next (decrease) Row (RS): Decrease 1 st at each Neck edge on the next row then every 4ᵗʰ row 4 times more — 16{18-18-20} sts each side.

Work even until Armholes measure 7{7¹/₂-8-8¹/₂}"/ 18{19-20.5-21.5} cm, end WS.

Shoulder Shaping (RS): Bind off 8{9-9-10} sts from each shoulder edge 2 times.

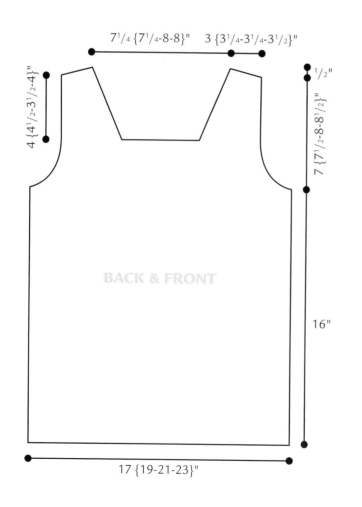

7¹/₄ {7¹/₄-8-8}"   3 {3¹/₄-3¹/₄-3¹/₂}"

4 {4¹/₂-3¹/₂-4}"

¹/₂"

7 {7¹/₂-8-8¹/₂}"

BACK & FRONT

16"

17 {19-21-23}"

FINISHING

Sew Front to Back at shoulders. Sew side seams *(Fig. 16, page 127)*.

Armhole Trim: With circular needle and RS facing, beginning at underarm seam, pick up 80{84-88-92} sts evenly around Armhole *(Figs. 15a & b, page 127)*; place marker and join.

P1 rnd.

Bind off all sts in knit.

Neckline Trim: With circular needle and RS facing, beginning at left shoulder seam, * pick up 17{19-15-17} sts along Left Front Neck, 24{24-26-26} sts along center Front Neck edge, 17{19-15-17} sts along Right Front Neck edge; rep from * for back; place marker and join — 116{124-112-120} sts.

P1 rnd.

Bind off all sts in knit AND AT THE SAME TIME, K2 tog at the 4 Neck corners.

Aztec Inspiration
A FAMILY OF SWEATERS

✳ ✳ ✳ ✳ ✳ ✳ ✳ ✳ ✳ ✳ ✳ ✳ ✳ ✳ ✳ ✳ ✳ ✳ ✳

In SAUCY yarn from JCA
Man's Vest • Woman's Cardigan • Child's Pullover

I have enjoyed reading about the Aztec and Mayan cultures over the years, and this group of family sweaters is a nod to that fascination of mine. The knit/purl triangular motifs resemble the ancient towering pyramid-like structures, and the other rippled pattern stitch stands for the huge banks of steps that lead up to the pinnacles.

I chose the colors of a wild zinnia for the woman's main color (a flower that the Aztecs grew), tempered with summer cocoa (another Aztec item), touched with Aztec gold! For the man's vest, the jungle green has glints of the riches of turquoise and gold. The child's sweater shares these bright colors, tipped with sporty stripes.

Each sweater shares the same easy patterns, but placed in a different way. Any of these sweaters could become a staple summer item if worked in a solid color as well. All are easy to make with simple shapes and easy-to-wear raglans for woman and child.

Here the 100% cotton holds color strong and bright, with the cooling effect of a slight sheen. Should you want sweaters that are more "trans-seasonal," as we say in the rag trade, you could make them in a wool or wool blend, fuzzier or less body skimming.

Instructions begin on page 106.

PATTERN STITCHES
(For All Sweaters)

K1/P1 RIB: Multiple of 2 sts plus 1
Row 1 (RS): K2, * P1, K1; rep from * across to last st, K1.
Row 2 (WS): P2, * K1, P1; rep from * across to last st, P1.
Rep Rows 1 and 2 for K1/P1 Rib.

STOCKINETTE STITCH
(St st): Any number of sts
Knit on RS, purl on WS.

ADULT PYRAMID PATTERN:
Multiple of 8 sts plus 1
Rows 1 and 3 (RS): P1, * K1, P1; rep from * across.
Rows 2 and 4 (WS): K1, * P1, K1; rep from * across.
Rows 5 and 7: P1, * (P1, K1) 3 times, P2; rep from * across.
Rows 6 and 8: K1, * (K1, P1) 3 times, K2; rep from * across.
Rows 9 and 11: P1, * P2, K1, P1, K1, P3; rep from * across.
Rows 10 and 12: K1, * K2, P1, K1, P1, K3; rep from * across.
Rows 13 and 15: P1, * P3, K1, P4; rep from * across.
Rows 14 and 16: K1, * K3, P1, K4; rep from * across.
Row 17: K1 MC, * K1 CC1, K1 MC; rep from * across.
Row 18: P1 MC, * P1 CC1, P1 MC; rep from * across.
Rows 19-34: Rep Rows 1-16.
Row 35: K1 MC, * K1 CC2, K1 MC; rep from * across.
Row 36: P1 MC, * P1 CC2, P1 MC; rep from * across.
Rep Rows 1-36 for Pyramid Pattern.

CHILD'S PYRAMID PATTERN:
Multiple of 8 sts plus 1
Rows 1 and 3 (RS): P1, * K1, P1; rep from * across.
Rows 2 and 4 (WS): K1, * P1, K1; rep from * across.
Rows 5 and 7: P1, * (P1, K1) 3 times, P2; rep from * across.
Rows 6 and 8: K1, * (K1, P1) 3 times, K2; rep from * across.
Rows 9 and 11: P1, * P2, K1, P1, K1, P3; rep from * across.
Rows 10 and 12: K1, * K2, P1, K1, P1, K3; rep from * across.
Rows 13 and 15: P1, * P3, K1, P4; rep from * across.
Rows 14 and 16: K1, * K3, P1, K4; rep from * across.
Row 17: K1 MC, * P1 CC, K1 MC; rep from * across.
Row 18: P1 MC, * P1 CC, P1 MC; rep from * across.
Rep Rows 1-18 for Pyramid Pattern.

TEXTURED PATTERN: Multiple of 3 sts
Rows 1 and 3 (RS): Knit across.
Rows 2 and 4: Purl across.
Rows 5 and 7: K1, * P1, K2; rep from * across to last 2 sts, P1, K1.
Rows 6 and 8: P1, * K1, P2; rep from * across to last 2 sts, K1, P1.
Rows 9 and 11: * P2, K1; rep from * across.
Rows 10 and 12: * P1, K2; rep from * across.
Rep Rows 1-12 for Textured Pattern.

Man's VEST

SIZES

To fit sizes Small {Medium-Large-Extra Large-Extra Extra Large}
Sample in size Medium.

MEASUREMENTS

Finished chest at underarm: 36{39-42-46-49}"/91.5{99-106.5-117-124.5} cm
Length to shoulder: 25$\frac{1}{2}${26-26$\frac{1}{2}$-27-27$\frac{1}{2}$}"/65{66-67.5-68.5-70} cm

Size Note: Instructions are written for size Small with sizes Medium, Large, X-Large
and XX-Large in braces { }. Instructions will be easier to read if you circle all the
numbers pertaining to your size. If only one number is given, it applies to all sizes.

MATERIALS

REYNOLDS/JCA "Saucy"
(100% Mercerized Cotton;
100 grams/185 yards)
  (MC): Color #960 (Jungle Green):
    5{5-6-6-7} skeins
  (CC1): Color #405 (Gold): 1 skein
  (CC2): Color #117 (Turquoise): 1 skein
Straight knitting needles, sizes 7 (4.5 mm) **and**
  8 (5 mm) **or** size needed to obtain gauge
24" (61 cm) Circular needle, size 7 (4.5 mm)

GAUGE

Over Pyramid Pattern using larger needles:
20 sts and 24 rows = 4" (10 cm)
Over Textured Pattern using larger needles:
19 sts and 24 rows = 4" (10 cm)

Techniques used:
• K2 tog *(Fig. 4, page 123)*
• SSK *(Figs. 7a-c, page 124)*

Note: Refer to Pattern Stitches, page 106.

Instructions begin on page 108.

BACK

With smaller needles and CC2, cast on 93{101-109-117-125} sts.

Work in K1/P1 Rib for 2 rows. Change to MC and continue in K1/P1 Rib until piece measures 2¹/₂" (6.5 cm), end WS.

Change to larger needles.

Establish Patterns (RS):

K2 (edge sts), work in Pyramid Pattern to last 2 sts, K2 (edge sts).

Keeping 2 edge sts each side in St st, work in Pyramid Pattern as established until piece measures 15¹/₂" (39.5 cm), end WS.

Armhole Shaping (RS):

Bind off 3 sts at the beginning of the next 6 rows — 75{83-91-99-107} sts.

Keeping 1 edge st each side in St st, work as established until Armholes measure 10{10¹/₂-11-11¹/₂-12}"/ 25.5{26.5-28-29-30.5} cm, end WS.

Shoulder and Back Neck Shaping (RS):
Mark center 25{27-27-29-31} sts. Bind off 5{6-8-9-10} sts, work across to marker; join a second ball of yarn and bind off center 25{27-27-29-31} sts, work to end.

Working both sides at the same time, continue to bind off 5{6-8-9-10} sts at the beginning of the next 5{5-1-1-1} row(s), then 0{0-7-8-9} sts at the beginning of the next 4 rows *(see Zeros, page 121)* AND AT THE SAME TIME, bind off at each Neck edge 5 sts twice.

FRONT

Work as for Back through Armhole Shaping, end WS — 75{83-91-99-107} sts.

V-Neck Shaping (RS):
Mark center st. Work across to 3 sts before marker, K2 tog, K1; join a second ball of yarn, bind off center marked st, SSK, work to end of row.

Working both sides at the same time and keeping in pattern, continue to decrease at Neck edge every 2nd row 15{17-17-19-21} times, then every 4th row 6{5-5-4-3} times — 15{18-22-25-28} sts each side.

Work even until Armhole measures same as Back to Shoulder Shaping.

Shoulder Shaping (RS):
Working both sides at the same time, bind off 5{6-8-9-10} sts at the beginning of the next 6{6-2-2-2} rows, then 0{0-7-8-9} sts at the beginning of next 4 rows.

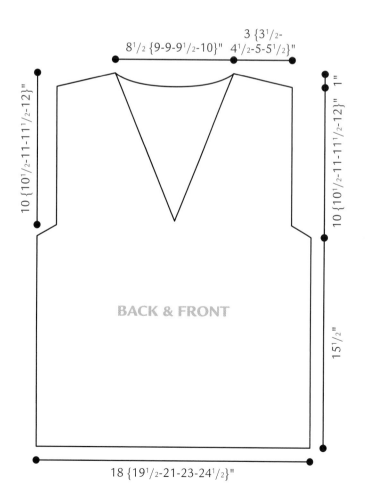

8¹/₂ {9-9-9¹/₂-10}"
3 {3¹/₂-4¹/₂-5-5¹/₂}"

10 {10¹/₂-11-11¹/₂-12}"

10 {10¹/₂-11-11¹/₂-12}" 1"

15¹/₂"

BACK & FRONT

18 {19¹/₂-21-23-24¹/₂}"

FINISHING

Sew Back to Front at shoulders.

Neck Finishing: With circular needle, MC and RS facing, beginning at lower right V-Neck, pick up 45{47-49-51-53} sts along Right Front Neck edge *(Figs. 15a & b, page 127)*, 38{40-40-42-44} sts along Back Neck, then 45{47-49-51-53} sts along Left Front Neck edge; do not join — 128{134-138-144-150} sts.

Working back and forth, knit 3 rows.
Change to CC2 and knit 1 row.

Bind off all sts in knit.

Overlap fronts where they meet at lower V-Neck and sew in place.

Armhole Finishing: With smaller needles, MC and RS facing, pick up 91{95-99-103-107} sts evenly along Armhole edge.

Knit 1 row.
Change to CC2 and knit 1 row.

Bind off all sts in knit.

Repeat for second Armhole.

Sew side seams *(Fig. 16, page 127)*. ✳

Woman's CARDIGAN

SIZES

To fit sizes Small {Medium-Large-Extra Large}
Sample in size Medium.

MEASUREMENTS

Finished Bust at underarm: 34{37-40-44}"/86.5{94-101.5-112} cm
Length to back neck, below finishing: 13^1/$_2${14-14^1/$_2$-15}"/34.5{35.5-37-38} cm
Sleeve width at upper arm: 12{12^1/$_2$-13^1/$_2$-15}"/30.5{32-34.5-38} cm

Size Note: Instructions are written for size Small with sizes Medium, Large
and X-Large in braces { }. Instructions will be easier to read if you circle all the
numbers pertaining to your size. If only one number is given, it applies to all sizes.

MATERIALS

REYNOLDS/JCA "Saucy" (4 MEDIUM)
(100% Mercerized Cotton;
100 grams/185 yards)
  (MC): Color #125 (Zinnia Red):
    2{2-2-3} skeins
  (CC1): Color #736 (Cocoa):
    3{3-3-4} skeins
  (CC2): Color #405 (Gold): 1 skein
Straight knitting needles, size 7 (4.5 mm) **and**
  8 (5 mm) **or** size needed to obtain gauge
1^3/$_8$" (35 mm) Button

GAUGE

Over Pyramid Pattern using larger needles:
20 sts and 24 rows = 4" (10 cm)
Over Textured Pattern using larger needles:
19 sts and 24 rows = 4" (10 cm)
Take time to save time, check your gauge.

Techniques used:
• K2 tog *(Fig. 4, page 123)*
• SSK *(Figs. 7a-c, page 124)*

Note: Refer to Pattern Stitches, page 106.

Instructions begin on page 112.

BACK
Using CC1 and smaller needles, cast on
103{111-119-129} sts.

Work in K1/P1 Rib for 1/2"
(12 mm), end RS.
Change to MC and purl WS row decreasing 10{10-10-12} sts evenly across *(see Increasing or Decreasing Evenly Across A Row, page 123)* —
93{101-109-117} sts.

Change to larger needles.

Establish Patterns (RS): K2 (edge sts), work in Pyramid Pattern to last 2 sts, K2 (edge sts).

Keeping 2 edge sts each side in St st, work as established until 2 rep of Pyramid Pattern are complete
[36 rows, piece measures approximately 6 1/2"
(16.5 cm)], end WS.

Change to CC1 keeping 2 edge sts each side in St st, work Row 1 of Textured Pattern AND AT THE SAME TIME decrease 8{10-12-11} sts evenly across — 85{91-97-106} sts.

Continue Textured Pattern and work until piece measures 10" (25.5 cm) from beginning, end WS.

Raglan Armhole Shaping (RS): Bind off 5 sts at the beginning of the next 2 rows.

Next (decrease) Row (RS): K1, SSK, work in pattern to last 3 sts, K2 tog, K1.

Keeping 2 edge sts each side in St st, rep decrease row every RS row 10{11-13-13} times more.

Bind off 2 sts at the beginning of the next 0{0-0-2} rows *(see Zeros, page 121)*.

Bind off remaining 53{57-59-64} sts.

LEFT FRONT
Using CC1 and smaller needles, cast on 53{59-61-67} sts.

Work in K1/P1 Rib for 1/2"
(12 mm), end RS.
Change to MC and purl WS row decreasing 6 sts evenly across —
47{53-55-61} sts.

Change to larger needles.

Establish Patterns (RS): K2 (edge sts), P1{0-1-0}, K1{0-1-0}, work Row 1 of Pyramid Pattern to last 2 sts, K2 (edge sts).

Next Row (WS): P2, work Row 2 of Pyramid Pattern to last 4{2-4-2} sts, P1{0-1-0}, K1{0-1-0}, P2.

Keeping 2 edge sts each side in St st, work as established until 2 reps of Pyramid Pattern are complete [36 rows, piece measures approximately 6 1/2" (16.5 cm)], end WS.

Change to CC1 and keeping 2 edge sts each side in St st, work Row 1 of Textured Pattern AND AT THE SAME TIME decrease 4{7-6-6} sts evenly across — 43{46-49-55} sts.

Continue Textured Pattern and work until piece measures 10" (25.5 cm) from beginning, end WS.

Raglan Armhole Shaping (RS): Bind off 5 sts at the beginning of the row — 38{41-44-50} sts.

Next (decrease) Row (RS): K1, SSK, work in pattern to end — 37{40-43-49} sts.

Keeping 2 edge sts each side in St st, rep decrease row every RS row 4{6-7-7} times more — 33{34-36-42} sts.

Bind off 2 sts at the beginning of the next 3{2-3-4} RS rows — 27{30-30-34} sts.

Bind off remaining 27{30-30-34} sts.

RIGHT FRONT

Work as for Left Front, reversing all patterns and shaping.

RIGHT SLEEVE

Using CC1 and smaller size needles, cast on 77{81-89-99} sts.

Work in K1/P1 Rib for $\frac{1}{2}$" (12 mm), end RS.
Change to MC and purl WS row decreasing 8{8-10-10} sts evenly across — 69{73-79-89} sts.

Change to larger needles.

Establish Pattern (RS):
K2 (edge sts), P 0{1-1-1}, K 0{1-0-1}, work Row 1 of Pyramid Pattern to last 2{4-3-4} sts, K 0{1-0-1}, P 0{1-1-1}, K2 (edge sts).

Next Row (WS): P2, K 0{1-1-1}, P 0{1-0-1}, work Row 2 of Pyramid Pattern to last 2{4-3-4} sts, P 0{1-0-1}, K 0{1-1-1}, P2.

Keeping 2 edge sts each side in St st, work as established until one rep of Pyramid Pattern is complete [18 rows, piece measures approximately 3$\frac{1}{2}$" (9 cm)], end WS.

Change to CC1 and keeping 2 edge sts each side in St st, work Row 1 of Textured Pattern AND AT THE SAME TIME decrease 11{12-12-16} sts evenly across — 58{61-67-73} sts.

Continue Textured Pattern and work until piece measures 7" (18 cm) from beginning, end WS.

Raglan Cap Shaping (RS):
Bind off 5 sts at beginning of the next 2 rows — 48{51-57-63} sts.

Next (decrease) Row (RS):
K1, SSK, work in pattern to last 3 sts, K2 tog, K1 — 46{49-55-61} sts.

Keeping 2 edge sts each side in St st, rep decrease at BEGINNING of RS rows every 4th{4th-4th-2nd} row 3{3-2-11} times, then every RS row 1{2-6-0} time(s) AND AT THE SAME TIME, rep decrease at END of RS rows every 6th{6th-4th-4th} row 2{1-5-3} time(s), then every 4th{4th-2nd-2nd} row 2{4-3-8} times.

Work until decreases at beginning of RS rows are completed.

Top of Cap (RS): Bind off 9 sts at beginning of RS rows 2{1-1-1} time(s), then 10 sts 2{3-3-3} times AND AT THE SAME TIME continue to decrease at end of RS row as described.

LEFT SLEEVE

Work as for Right Sleeve, reversing Raglan Cap Shaping.

FINISHING

Sew Fronts to Back to Sleeves at Raglan seams (*Fig. 16, page 127*).
Sew side and Sleeve seams.

Neck Finishing: With smaller needles, MC and RS facing, beginning at Right Front Neck edge, pick up 23{25-25-27} sts along Right Front Neck edge (*Figs. 15a & b, page 127*), 31 sts along Sleeve top, 41{45-47-51} sts along Back Neck edge, 31 sts along second Sleeve top, then 23{25-25-27} sts along Left Front Neck edge — 149{157-159-167} sts.

Knit 3 rows.
Change to CC2 and knit 1 row.

Knit next row decreasing 21 sts evenly spaced — 128{136-138-146} sts.

Change to CC1 and knit 7 rows.

Bind off in knit on next row AND AT THE SAME TIME decrease 13{13-11-13} sts evenly spaced.

Instructions continued on page 114.

Left Front Button Band:
With smaller needles, MC and RS facing, pick up 59{61-63-65} sts evenly spaced along Left Front.

Knit 3 rows.

Bind off all sts in knit.

Right Front Band: With smaller needles, CC1 and RS facing, pick up 59{61-63-65} sts evenly spaced along Right Front.

Next (buttonhole) Row (WS):
K 10, make a 5-st buttonhole (by bind off 5 sts and casting on 5 sts while working bind off row), knit to end.

Knit 2 rows.

Bind off all sts in knit.

Sew button opposite buttonhole. ✳

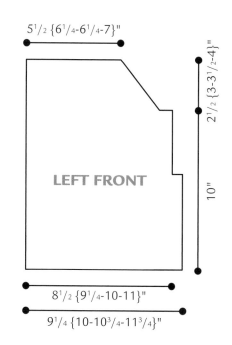

5¹/₂ {6¹/₄-6¹/₄-7}"

2¹/₂ {3-3¹/₂-4}"

10"

LEFT FRONT

8¹/₂ {9¹/₄-10-11}"

9¹/₄ {10-10³/₄-11³/₄}"

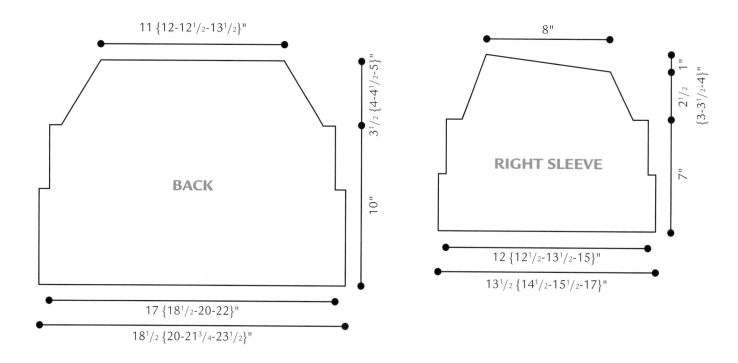

11 {12-12¹/₂-13¹/₂}"

3¹/₂ {4-4¹/₂-5}"

10"

BACK

17 {18¹/₂-20-22}"

18¹/₂ {20-21³/₄-23¹/₂}"

8"

1"

2¹/₂ {3-3¹/₂-4}"

7"

RIGHT SLEEVE

12 {12¹/₂-13¹/₂-15}"

13¹/₂ {14¹/₂-15¹/₂-17}"

Child's PULLOVER

SIZES
To fit Child's sizes 6{8-10}
Sample in size 8.

MEASUREMENTS
Finished Chest: 27{30-33}"/68.5{76-84} cm
Length: 18{18^1/$_2$-19^1/$_2$}"/45.5{47-49.5} cm
Sleeve width at upper arm: 11{12-13}"/28{30.5-33} cm

Size Note: Instructions are written for size 6 with sizes 8 and 10 in braces { }. Instructions will be easier to read if you circle all the numbers pertaining to your size. If only one number is given, it applies to all sizes.

✳ ✳

MATERIALS
REYNOLDS/JCA "Saucy" [MEDIUM 4]
(100% Mercerized Cotton;
100 grams/185 yards)
   (MC): Color #117 (Turquoise):
      4{4-5} skeins
   (CC): Color #405 (Gold): 1 skein
Straight knitting needles, sizes 7 (4.5 mm) **and**
   8 (5 mm) **or** sizes needed to obtain gauge
24" (61 cm) Circular needle, size 7 (4.5 mm)
Marker

GAUGE
Over Pyramid Pattern using larger needles:
20 sts and 24 rows = 4" (10 cm)
Over Textured Pattern using larger needles:
19 sts and 24 rows = 4" (10 cm)
Take time to save time, check your gauge.

Techniques used:
• K2 tog *(Fig. 4, page 123)*
• SSK *(Figs. 7a-c, page 124)*
• M1 *(Figs. 3a & b, page 123)*

Note: Refer to Pattern Stitches, page 106.

Instructions begin on page 116.

BACK

With smaller needles and CC, cast on 69{77-85} sts.

Work in K1/P1 Rib for 2 rows. Change to MC and continue in K1/P1 Rib until piece measures 2" (5 cm), end WS.

Change to larger needles.

Establish Patterns (RS): K2 (edge sts), work in Pyramid Pattern to last 2 sts, K2 (edge sts).

Keeping 2 edge sts each side in St st, work as established until piece measures 11" (28 cm), end WS.

Raglan Armhole Shaping (RS): Bind off 5{6-6} sts at the beginning of the next 2 rows, then 0{0-2} sts at the beginning of the next 0{0-4} rows *(see Zeros, page 121)* — 59{65-65} sts.

Next (decrease) Row (RS): K1, SSK, work in pattern as established to last 3 sts, K2 tog, K1 — 57{63-63} sts.

Rep decrease row every other row 12{14-14} times — 33{35-35} sts.

Bind off remaining 33{35-35} sts.

FRONT

With smaller needles and CC, cast on 69{77-85} sts.

Work in K1/P1 Rib for 2 rows. Change to MC and continue in K1/P1 Rib until piece measures 2" (5 cm), end WS.

Change to larger needles.

Establish Patterns (RS): K2 (edge sts), work in Pyramid Pattern to last 2 sts, K2 (edge sts).

Keeping 2 edge sts each side in St st, work as established until piece measures 11" (28 cm), end WS.

Raglan Armhole Shaping (RS): Bind off 5{6-6} sts at the beginning of the next 2 rows, then 0{0-2} sts at the beginning of next 0{0-4} rows — 59{65-65} sts.

Next (decrease) Row (RS): K1, SSK, work in pattern as established to last 3 sts, K2 tog, K1 — 57{63-63} sts.

Rep decrease row every other row 9{11-11} times — 39{41-41} sts.

Bind off remaining 39{41-41} sts.

RIGHT SLEEVE

With smaller needles and CC, cast on 33{33-33} sts.

[K2 rows CC, K2 rows MC] 3 times, increasing 4 sts evenly on last WS row *(see Increasing or Decreasing Evenly Across a Row, page 123)* — 37{37-37} sts.

Change to larger needles.

Establish Patterns (RS): K2 (edge sts), work in Textured Pattern to last 2 sts, K2 (edge sts).

Keeping 2 edge sts each side in St st, work WS row.

Next (increase) Row (RS): K2, M1, work in pattern to last 2 sts, M1, K2 — 39{39-39} sts.

Working increases into Textured Pattern, rep increase row every 8th{6th-6th} row 5{5-10} times, then every 10th{8th-8th} row 2{4-1} time(s) — 53{57-61} sts.

Work even until Sleeve measures 13{13$\frac{1}{2}$-14$\frac{1}{2}$}"/ 33{34.5-37} cm or to desired length, end WS.

Raglan Cap Shaping (RS): Bind off 5{6-6} sts at beginning of next 2 rows — 43{45-49} sts.

Next (decrease) Row (RS): K1, SSK, work in pattern to last 3 sts, K2 tog, K1 — 41{43-47} sts.

Work decreases as described at BEGINNING of RS rows every 4th row 0{1-1} time(s), then every 2nd row 9{9-11} times AND at the END of RS rows every 4th row 3{4-4} times, then every 2nd row 3{3-5} times — 26 sts.

Work WS row.

Instructions continued on page 118.

Top of Cap (RS):
Bind off at the beginning of the RS rows 5 sts once, then 6 sts 3 times AND AT THE SAME TIME, decrease 1 st at end of RS rows 3 times more.

LEFT SLEEVE

Work as for Right Sleeve to Raglan Cap Shaping.

Raglan Cap Shaping (RS):
Bind off 5{6-6} sts at beginning of next 2 rows — 43{45-49} sts.

Next (decrease) Row (RS):
K1, SSK, work in pattern to last 3 sts, K2 tog, K1 — 41{43-47} sts.

Work decreases as described at BEGINNING of RS rows every 4th row 3{4-4} times, then every 2nd row 3{3-5} times and at the END of RS rows every 4th row 0{1-1} time(s), then every 2nd row 9{9-11} times — 26 sts.

Work WS row.

Top of Cap (RS):
Decrease 1 st at beginning of RS rows 3 times more AND AT THE SAME TIME, bind off at beginning of WS rows, 5 sts once, then 6 sts 3 times.

FINISHING

Sew Front to Back and Sleeves at Raglan seams *(Fig. 16, page 127)*.
Sew side and Sleeve seams.

Neck Finishing: With circular needle, CC and RS facing, beginning at right shoulder, pick up 25{27-27} sts along Back Neck edge *(Figs. 15a & b, page 127)*, 18 sts along Sleeve top, 30{32-32} sts along Front edge and 18 sts along second Sleeve top; place marker and join — 91{95-95} sts.

P1 rnd.
Change to MC, K1 rnd, P1 rnd.
Change to CC, K1 rnd, P1 rnd, K1 rnd.

Bind off all sts in knit. ✳

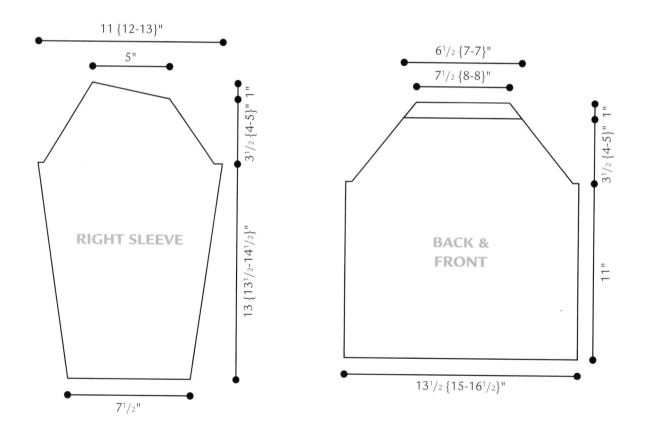

General
INSTRUCTIONS

✳ ✳ ✳ ✳ ✳ ✳ ✳ ✳ ✳ ✳ ✳ ✳ ✳ ✳ ✳ ✳ ✳ ✳

ABBREVIATIONS

cm	centimeters
cn	cable needle
dpn(s)	double-pointed needle(s)
K	knit
LH	Left Hand
LT	Left Twist
M1	Make one
mm	millimeters
P	purl
PM	place marker
PSSO	pass slipped stitch over
P2SSO	pass 2 slipped stitches over
rep	repeat
RH	Right Hand
Rnd(s)	Round(s)

RS	Right Side
RT	Right Twist
S4K	slip 4 seperately, knit 4 together
SSK	slip, slip, knit
st(s)	stitch(es)
tbl	through back loop(s)
tog	together
WS	Wrong Side
wyib	with yarn in back
wyif	with yarn in front
YO	yarn over(s)

* — work instructions following * as many **more** times as indicated in addition to the first time.

( ) or [ ] — work enclosed instructions **as many** times as specified by the number immediately following **or** work all enclosed instructions in the stitch indicated **or** contains explanatory remarks.

long dash — the number(s) given after a long dash (—) at the end of a row or round denote(s) the number of stitches you should have on that row or round.

work even — work without increasing or decreasing in the established pattern.

✳ ✳ ✳ ✳ ✳ ✳ ✳ ✳ ✳ ✳ ✳ ✳ ✳ ✳ ✳ ✳ ✳ ✳ ✳

KNIT TERMINOLOGY	
UNITED STATES	**INTERNATIONAL**
gauge =	tension
bind off =	cast off
yarn over (YO) =	yarn forward (yfwd) **or**
	yarn around needle (yrn)

Yarn Weight Symbol & Names	LACE 0	SUPER FINE 1	FINE 2	LIGHT 3	MEDIUM 4	BULKY 5	SUPER BULKY 6
Type of Yarns in Category	Fingering, size 10 crochet thread	Sock, Fingering, Baby	Sport, Baby	DK, Light Worsted	Worsted, Afghan, Aran	Chunky, Craft, Rug	Bulky, Roving
Knit Gauge Range* in Stockinette St to 4" (10 cm)	33-40** sts	27-32 sts	23-26 sts	21-24 sts	16-20 sts	12-15 sts	6-11 sts
Advised Needle Size Range	000-1	1 to 3	3 to 5	5 to 7	7 to 9	9 to 11	11 and larger

*GUIDELINES ONLY: The chart above reflects the most commonly used gauges and needle sizes for specific yarn categories.

** Lace weight yarns are usually knitted on larger needles to create lacy openwork patterns. Accordingly, a gauge range is difficult to determine. Always follow the gauge stated in your pattern.

KNITTING NEEDLES																
U.S.	0	1	2	3	4	5	6	7	8	9	10	10½	11	13	15	17
U.K.	13	12	11	10	9	8	7	6	5	4	3	2	1	00	000	---
Metric - mm	2	2.25	2.75	3.25	3.5	3.75	4	4.5	5	5.5	6	6.5	8	9	10	12.75

■□□□ **BEGINNER**	Projects for first-time knitters using basic knit and purl stitches. Minimal shaping.
■■□□ **EASY**	Projects using basic stitches, repetitive stitch patterns, simple color changes, and simple shaping and finishing.
■■■□ **INTERMEDIATE**	Projects with a variety of stitches, such as basic cables and lace, simple intarsia, double-pointed needles and knitting in the round needle techniques, mid-level shaping and finishing.
■■■■ **EXPERIENCED**	Projects using advanced techniques and stitches, such as short rows, fair isle, more intricate intarsia, cables, lace patterns, and numerous color changes.

GAUGE

Exact gauge is **essential** for proper fit. Before beginning your project, make a sample swatch in the yarn and needles specified. After completing the swatch, measure it, counting your stitches and rows carefully. If your swatch is larger or smaller than specified, **make another, changing needle size to get the correct gauge**. Keep trying until you find the size needles that will give you the specified gauge. Once proper gauge is obtained, measure width of garment approximately every 3" (7.5 cm) to be sure gauge remains consistent.

If you have more rows per inch than specified, perhaps using a larger size needle for the purl rows would correct the gauge; if fewer, perhaps using a smaller size needle for the purl rows would correct the gauge.

HINTS

As in all garments, good finishing techniques make a big difference in the quality of the piece. Do not tie knots. Always start a new ball at the beginning of a row, leaving ends long enough to weave in later. With **wrong** side facing, weave the needle through several stitches, then reverse the direction and weave it back through several stitches. When the ends are secure, clip them off close to work.

ZEROS

To consolidate the length of an involved pattern, Zeros are sometimes used so that all sizes can be combined. For example, knit 0{1-2} sts means the first size would do nothing, the second size would K1, and the largest size would K2.

MARKERS

As a convenience to you, we have used markers to help distinguish the beginning of a pattern or round or to mark placement of decreases or increases. Place a marker as instructed. You may use purchased markers or tie a length of contrasting color yarn around the needle. When you reach a marker on each row or round, slip it from the left needle to the right needle; remove it when no longer needed.

BACKWARD LOOP CAST ON

Make a loop and place it on the needle (*Fig. 1*).

Fig. 1

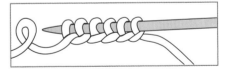

YARN OVERS

A yarn over *(abbreviated YO)* is simply placing the yarn over the right needle creating an extra stitch. Since the yarn over produces a hole in the knit fabric, it is used for a lacy effect. On the row following a yarn over, you must be careful to keep it on the needle and treat it as a stitch by knitting or purling it as instructed.

To make a yarn over, you'll loop the yarn over the needle like you would to knit or purl a stitch, bringing it either to the front or to the back of the piece so that it'll be ready to work the next stitch, creating a new stitch on the needle as follows:

After a knit stitch, before a knit stitch

Bring the yarn forward **between** the needles, then back **over** the top of the right hand needle, so that it is now in position to knit the next stitch *(Fig. 2a)*.

Fig. 2a

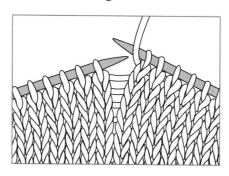

After a purl stitch, before a purl stitch

Take the yarn **over** the right hand needle to the back, then forward **under** it, so that it is now in position to purl the next stitch *(Fig. 2b)*.

Fig. 2b

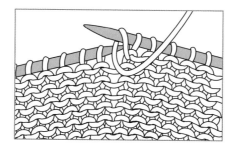

After a knit stitch, before a purl stitch

Bring the yarn forward between the needles, then back **over** the top of the right hand needle and forward **between** the needles again, so that it is now in position to purl the next stitch *(Fig. 2c)*.

Fig. 2c

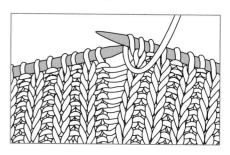

After a purl stitch, before a knit stitch

Take the yarn **over** the right hand needle to the back, so that it is now in position to knit the next stitch *(Fig. 2d)*.

Fig. 2d

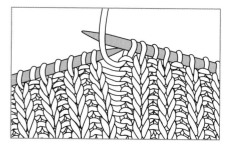

INCREASE
MAKE 1 (abbreviated M1)

Insert the left needle under the horizontal strand between the stitches from the **front (Fig. 3a)**, then knit into the **back** of the strand **(Fig. 3b)**.

Fig. 3a

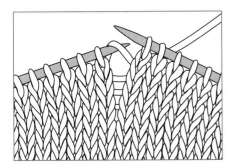

Fig. 3b

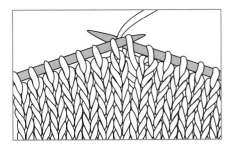

INCREASING OR DECREASING EVENLY ACROSS A ROW

Add one to the number of increases/decreases required and divide that number into the number of stitches on the needle. Subtract one from the result and the new number is the approximate number of stitches to be worked between each increase/decrease. Adjust the number as needed.

DECREASES
KNIT 2 TOGETHER
(abbreviated K2 tog)

Insert the right needle into the front of the first two stitches on the left needle as if to **knit (Fig. 4)**, then **knit** them together as if they were one stitch.

Fig. 4

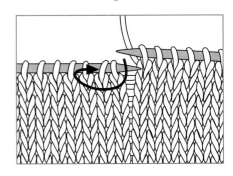

PURL 2 TOGETHER
(abbreviated P2 tog)

Insert the right needle into the **front** of the first two stitches on the left needle as if to **purl (Fig. 5)**, then **purl** them together as if they were one stitch.

Fig. 5

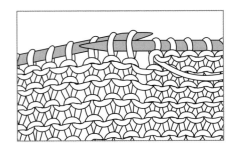

PURL 2 TOGETHER THROUGH THE BACK LOOP *(abbreviated P2 tog tbl)*

Insert the right needle into the **back** of both stitches from **back** to **front** *(Fig. 6)*, then purl them together as if they were one stitch.

Fig. 6

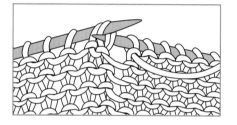

SLIP, SLIP, KNIT
(abbreviated SSK)

Separately slip two stitches as if to **knit** *(Fig. 7a)*. Insert the **left** needle into the **front** of both slipped stitches *(Fig. 7b)* and then **knit** them together as if they were one stitch *(Fig. 7c)*.

Fig. 7a

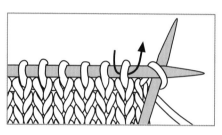

Fig. 7b

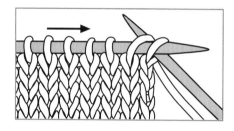

Fig. 7c

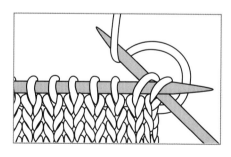

KNIT 3 TOGETHER
(abbreviated K3 tog)

Insert the right needle into the front of the first three stitches on the left needle as if to **knit** *(Fig. 8)*, then **knit** them together as if they were one stitch.

Fig. 8

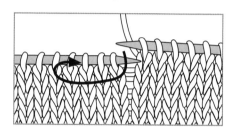

SLIP 1, KNIT 2 TOGETHER, PASS SLIPPED STITCH OVER

(abbreviated slip 1, K2 tog, PSSO)

Slip one stitch as if to **knit** *(Fig. 9a)*, then knit the next two stitches together *(Fig. 4, page 123)*. With the left needle bring the slipped stitch over the stitch just made *(Fig. 9b)* and off the needle.

Fig. 9a

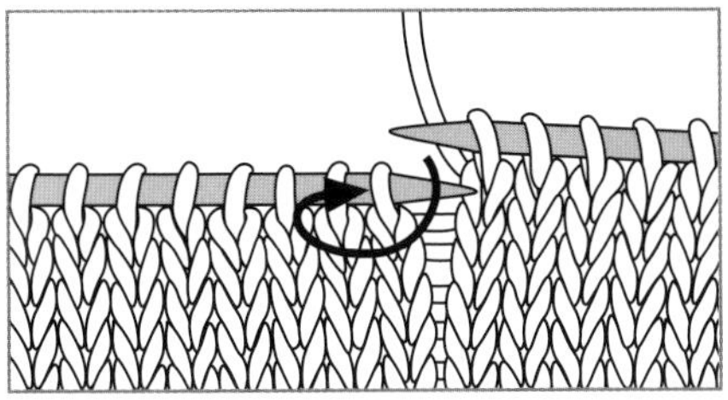

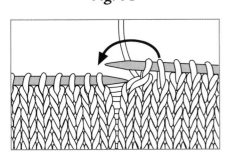

Fig. 9b

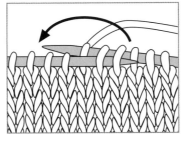

SLIP 2, KNIT 1, PASS 2 SLIPPED STITCHES OVER *(abbreviated slip 2, K1, P2SSO)*

Slip two stitches together as if to **knit** *(Fig. 10a)*, then knit the next stitch. With the left needle, bring both slipped stitches over the knit stitch *(Fig. 10b)* and off the needle.

Fig. 10a

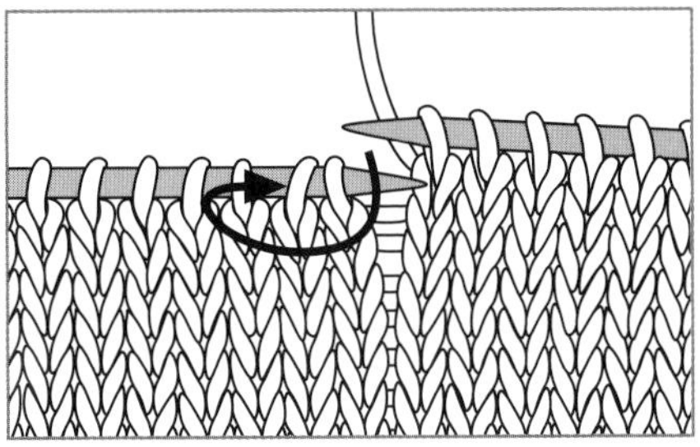

Fig. 10b

KNIT 4 TOGETHER

(abbreviated K4 tog)

Insert the right needle into the front of the first three stitches on the left needle as if to **knit** *(Fig. 11)*, then **knit** them together as if they were one stitch.

Fig. 11

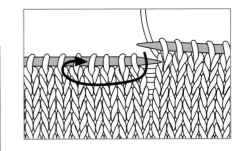

THROUGH BACK LOOP *(abbreviated tbl)*

When instructed to knit or purl into the back loop of a stitch *(Fig. 12)*, the result will be twisted stitches.

Fig. 12

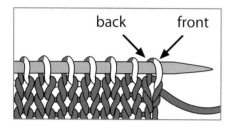

USING DOUBLE-POINTED NEEDLES

When working too few stitches to use a circular needle, double-pointed needles are required. Divide the stitches into fourths and slip one-fourth of the stitches onto each of 4 double-pointed needles *(Fig. 13)*, forming a square. With the fifth needle, knit across the stitches on the first needle. You will now have an empty needle with which to knit the stitches from the next needle. Work the first stitch of each needle firmly to prevent gaps.

Fig. 13

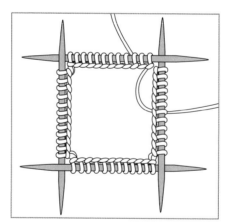

CHANGING COLORS

Wind small amounts of each color onto a bobbin to keep the different color yarns from tangling. You'll need one bobbin for each color change, except when there are so few stitches of the new color that it would be easier to carry the unused color **loosely** across the back *(Fig. 14)*. Always keep the bobbins on the **wrong** side of the garment. maintain gauge when following Charts.

Fig. 14

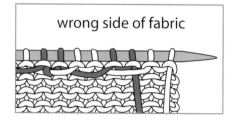

PICKING UP STITCHES

When instructed to pick up stitches, insert the needle from the **front** to the **back** under two strands at the edge of the worked piece *(Figs. 15a & b)*. Put the yarn around the needle as if to **knit**, then bring the needle with the yarn back through the stitch to the right side, resulting in a stitch on the needle.

Repeat this along the edge, picking up the required number of stitches.

A crochet hook may be helpful to pull yarn through.

Fig. 15a

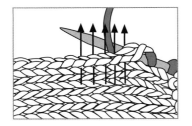

Fig. 15b

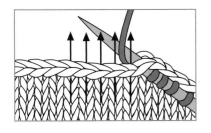

SEWING SEAMS

With the right side of both pieces facing you and edges even, sew through both sides once to secure the seam. Insert the needle under the bar **between** the first and second stitches on the row and pull the yarn through *(Fig. 16)*. Insert the needle under the next bar on the second side. Repeat From side to side, being careful to match rows. If the edges are different lengths, it may be necessary to insert the needle under two bars at one edge.

Fig. 16

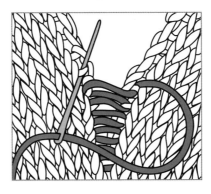

Acknowledgements

First of all, I would like to extend a heartfelt thanks to all the knitters who helped me with the projects in this book, and those who contributed to my other design work in order that I could complete this project. I could not do my job without them! Their attention to detail and skillfulness is deeply appreciated: Virginia Daving, Laura Folden, Lucinda Heller, Mireille Holland, Cheryl Mariolis, Lynn Marlow, Debbie O'Neille, Pat Yankee, and Fran Scullin.

A big thank you to my longtime colleague and dear friend Barbara Khouri, for all her technical help with the sizing and charts — as well as her expert knitting!

I am very grateful to the yarn companies who graciously and generously provided their wonderful yarns for this book of designs:
Berroco
Blue Sky Alpaca
Caron International
Classic Elite
JCA/Artful Yarns
Knit One Crochet Too
Manos Del Uruguay
Nashua Handknits
Rowan
Schulana (also suppliers of Louisa Harding)
Tahki-Stacy Charles

Thanks to my friends Sheila D'Ammassa and Sandy Pearlman for keeping me up to date on yarn and fashion trends, and for inspiring me with their own knitting interests.

Love and gratitude to Paul Di Filippo, my ever-supportive companion in life and work, without whom I would be nothing!

A grateful embrace to my editor Debra Nettles whose enthusiastic support has been a delight and an inspiration.

Warm Weather
KNITS BY DEBORAH NEWTON

A LEISURE ARTS PUBLICATION

EDITORIAL STAFF
Editor-in-Chief: Susan White Sullivan
Knit and Crochet Publications Director:
  Debra Nettles
Special Projects Director: Susan Frantz Wiles
Senior Prepress Director: Mark Hawkins
Art Publications Director: Rhonda Shelby
Technical Writer: Linda Daley
Editorial Writer: Susan McManus Johnson
Art Category Manager: Lora Puls
Graphic Designers: Becca Snider,
  Amy Temple, and Janie Marie Wright
Imaging Technician: Stephanie Johnson
Photography Manager: Katherine Laughlin
Contributing Photostylist: Angela Alexander
Contributing Photographer: Jason Masters
Publishing Systems Administrator:
  Becky Riddle
Mac Information Technology Specialist:
  Robert Young

BUSINESS STAFF
President and Chief Executive Officer:
  Rick Barton
Vice President and Chief Operations Officer:
  Tom Siebenmorgen
Director of Finance and Administration:
  Laticia Mull Dittrich
National Sales Director: Martha Adams
Information Technology Director:
  Hermine Linz
Controller: Francis Caple
Vice President, Operations: Jim Dittrich
Retail Customer Service Manager:
  Stan Raynor
Print Production Manager: Fred F. Pruss

Library of Congress Control Number:
2010930928

ISBN-13: 978-1-60900-010-3

Table of CONTENTS

✳   ✳   ✳   ✳   ✳   ✳   ✳   ✳   ✳   ✳   ✳   ✳   ✳

Warm Weather SWEATERS

Warm weather sweaters are not just cold weather sweaters knitted with lighter yarns and fibers! Shapes and details are different too, as I think you can see with these new designs.

I took the opportunity to use some favorite yarns as well as design with some new and exciting fibers I was — and you might be! — less familiar with. Here bamboo, soy, and hemp meet the more traditional summer cotton, linen, and blends. As a New Englander, I know that warm weather still calls for the occasional "cool-wool" sweater, as well as the lightest cover-up for a steamy August evening. In other parts of the country, where warm weather is more of a constant, the demand is for breathable, lightweight and cool-to-the-touch sweaters — some of the newer fibers are just perfect for meeting these needs. Everywhere today air-conditioned buildings call for light sweaters.

Color is a design feature for warm weather too. Neutrals as well as shades of green and blue — sand, plants and water — are always cool feeling and light. Many plant fibers have an opalescent sheen, which I find crisp and summery. And what would summer be without the bright shades of beach umbrellas and paper lanterns or the festive colors of the dahlias and other annual flowers and vines — and vegetables, too, to name a few?

As a designer, I find that lots of fun things go into creating a collection like this! The sweaters in this book draw upon all my personal interest and seasonal pleasures. As a long-time knitwear designer, I adore the search for new ways to use pattern stitches. And I am inspired by current fashion as well as the classics. I juggle my fascination for vintage clothing and old sewing patterns with a love for costumes from the movies of the 30's and 40's. I live for the summer — the colors and light of my beloved Rhode Island summer coastline, and the lively nautical Newport and rural Block Island where I visit every spring and summer. I am inspired by the colors of my favorite home grown flowers and vegetables, and I draw on memories of foreign vacations, as well as armchair travel from the pages of books and magazines.